U0647047

本书为浙江工业大学校人文社科后期资助项目“二语学习者多维度词汇知识学习模式研究”（项目编号：SKY-ZX-20220281）研究成果，并获浙江工业大学外国语学院学术专著出版资助

FLA 外国语言学及应用语言学研究丛书

Second Language Vocabulary Acquisition Research from a Cognitive Perspective

认知视角下的二语词汇习得模式研究

宋丽娟　著

ZHEJIANG UNIVERSITY PRESS
浙江大学出版社
·杭州·

图书在版编目（CIP）数据

认知视角下的二语词汇习得模式研究 = Second Language Vocabulary Acquisition Research from a Cognitive Perspective ： 英文 / 宋丽娟著. — 杭州 ： 浙江大学出版社，2023.6

ISBN 978-7-308-23639-3

Ⅰ. ①认… Ⅱ. ①宋… Ⅲ. ①第二语言－词汇－教学研究－英文 Ⅳ. ①H003

中国国家版本馆CIP数据核字(2023)第059296号

认知视角下的二语词汇习得模式研究
宋丽娟　著

责任编辑　田　慧
责任校对　曾　庆
封面设计　项梦怡
出版发行　浙江大学出版社
（杭州市天目山路148号　邮政编码　310007）
（网址：http：//www.zjupress.com）
排　　版　杭州林智广告有限公司
印　　刷　广东虎彩云印刷有限公司绍兴分公司
开　　本　710mm×1000mm　1/16
印　　张　14.75
字　　数　267千
版 印 次　2023年6月第1版　2023年6月第1次印刷
书　　号　ISBN 978-7-308-23639-3
定　　价　68.00元

Preface

This book aims to explore an effective way of L2 vocabulary acquisition from a cognitive perspective. Although many studies have been conducted to investigate L2 lexical acquisition from various angles, most of these studies have stayed at a relatively superficial level by comparing different vocabulary teaching methods, without probing into the cognitive modes involved in these instructional methods. Based on Skehan's (1998) Information Processing Model, the present study explores the respective roles of input and output processing in L2 vocabulary acquisition, compares the effectiveness of different cognitive modes on L2 word learning and retention, and constructs a cognitive mode which is most beneficial for L2 vocabulary acquisition.

This book consists of six chapters. Chapter 1 reviews the research background of L2 vocabulary acquisition, lists the problems in this research field, proposes the necessity and feasibility of interpreting L2 vocabulary acquisition from a cognitive perspective, and illustrates the theoretical significance of this book.

Chapter 2 explores some theories and concepts related to L2 vocabulary acquisition. The first part of this chapter is a brief introduction. The second part highlights the distinction between breadth and depth of word knowledge, and then introduces different definitions of depth of word knowledge, which are continuum-based, dimensional-based and mental-lexical-based depth of word knowledge. The corresponding assessing measures of three types of depth of word knowledge are also described in this part. The third part of this chapter briefly reviews theories on lexical competence and introduces three lexical competence frameworks proposed by different researchers.

Chapter 3 is a review of some basic cognitive theories closely related to L2 vocabulary acquisition, such as levels of processing, input hypothesis, and output hypothesis. According to the theory of levels of processing (Craik & Lockhart, 1972), memory is a dynamic activity of the mind which may be affected by different levels or degrees of information processing. The more elaborated the information is processed, the better it will be stored in one's mind. The theory of levels of processing presents a distinction between intentional and incidental word learning from a psychological perspective. It is suggested that successful vocabulary acquisition is not determined by whether a word is learned intentionally or not, but by the depth of encoding on the target word knowledge. Skehan's (1998) Information Processing Model and other theories or models of input and output processing are also reviewed in this chapter. In Skehan's (1998) Information Processing Model, input and output processing are regarded as two important stages in the information processing flow. At the input processing stage, there co-exist two representational systems: the rule-based system and exemplar-based system. These two representational systems entail different cognitive modes, which differ in their effectiveness in different learning contexts. The rule-based system relates to a deductive cognitive mode, while the exemplar-based system involves an inductive cognitive mode. There has been a long-term debate on the relative effects of two cognitive modes on language learning. Ellis (1994) holds that the rule-based deductive mode is more beneficial than the inductive mode in promoting the input salience; while other researchers insist that inductive learning is more effective when second language acquisition and retention are concerned (Matthews et al., 1989). In this book, it is hypothesized that the inductive mode is more efficient in input processing than the deductive mode. Output, another important factor in an information processing model, is also addressed in this chapter. The roles of output take on four aspects, which are consciousness-raising, restructuring, hypotheses-testing, and automatization (Swain, 1995).

Based on the review of related theories and empirical studies, five questions are addressed in this study:

1) Is the inductive cognitive mode more effective in input processing in L2 vocabulary acquisition than the deductive cognitive mode?

2) What factors may have impacts on input processing in L2 vocabulary acquisition?

3) What roles does output play in L2 vocabulary acquisition?

4) Does the output processing have its limitations in promoting L2 vocabulary acquisition?

5) Will the joint effort of input and output processing have a better effect on L2 vocabulary acquisition than the single effort of input or output processing?

This research adopts a combination of two experiments to investigate the roles of input and output processing in L2 vocabulary acquisition.

Chapter 4 gives a detailed account of Experiment 1 which aimed to explore the effectiveness of different input processing modes on L2 vocabulary acquisition. The experimental conditions, procedures, results and its related discussions will all be illustrated in this chapter.

Experiment 2 probed into the roles of output processing in L2 vocabulary acquisition. Co-effects of input and output processing on L2 vocabulary acquisition were also explored through this experiment.

Chapter 5 presents the detailed information of Experiment 2, including experimental procedures, results, and related discussions.

The last chapter is a summary of the major findings in this research, which are as follows:

1) Intentional learning, compared with incidental learning, is more efficient in providing sufficient and diversified instances and promoting word exposure frequency in a short period. Through elaborated encoding on the diversified instances, learners can achieve a deep understanding of target

word knowledge, entailing multiple dimensions. In contrast, learners in the incidental learning context distribute most of their attention to extracting word meaning from the context, and often ignore other dimensions of word knowledge, such as a word's formal or functional features. This word learning process, which solely focuses on one aspect of word knowledge, is far from being sufficient for word knowledge encoding and is ineffective for new word learning and retention.

2) The exemplar-based inductive mode, in comparison with the rule-based deductive cognition mode, is more beneficial for L2 vocabulary acquisition. The inductive learning context is more learner-centered for motivate learners to extract or generalize the target word knowledge from instances by themselves. It is also proved to be more effective to promote learners' learning motivation and autonomy.

3) Task demands, depth of elaboration or processing, and input presentation modes are three important factors which may impact the effectiveness of input processing in the L2 vocabulary acquisition process.

4) Output is of vital importance in enhancing L2 vocabulary acquisition. Roles of output in the L2 vocabulary acquisition lie in increasing cognitive involvement load, enhancing word knowledge elaboration, facilitating hypothesis testing, and promoting receptive-to-productive knowledge transition.

5) Input and output processing are two important stages in the L2 vocabulary acquisition process. The joint work of the inductive input processing and output can greatly enhance L2 word knowledge elaboration and internalization.

The theoretical significance of this book is also addressed in Chapter 6. This book adopts Skehan's (1998) Information Processing Model as its theoretical framework to study L2 vocabulary acquisition from a cognitive perspective. It also probes into the cognitive modes which serve as the foundation of different teaching methods but are often ignored in L2 vocabulary acquisition research field. Based on Swain's (1985, 1995) Output Hypothesis, the book investigates the specific roles and limitations of output in L2 vocabulary acquisition, enriches the existing theories related to the Output Hypothesis, and testifies to the significance of the Output Hypothesis in L2 vocabulary acquisition research field.

Limitations of the present study and recommendations for future research are also discussed in Chapter 6. Firstly, the Vocabulary Knowledge Scale adopted in this research mainly focuses on tracking the development of word knowledge. However, it is far from enough to assess all aspects of word knowledge. Varied vocabulary assessing instruments are suggested to be adopted in future studies. Secondly, questionnaires and interviews are recommended to be used in future research to quantify the correlation between "attention" and "input processing".

CONTENTS

Chapter 4 An empirical study on input processing in L2 vocabulary acquisition

Chapter 5 An empirical study on output processing in L2 vocabulary acquisition

Chapter 6 Conclusion

List of Tables

List of Figures

Abbreviations

SLA	Second Language Acquisition
L1	First Language
L2	Second Language
VKS	Vocabulary Knowledge Scale
VLT	Vocabulary Levels Test
ANOVA	Analysis of Variation

Chapter 1 Introduction

1.1 Overview

The importance of vocabulary in Second Language Acquisition (SLA) has been widely discussed by researchers (Laufer, 1991; Meara, 1984; McCarthy, 1990; Vermeer, 1992; Gass & Selinker, 1994). It is claimed that vocabulary is the building block of all four language skills: reading, listening, writing and speaking. Some SLA researchers even give priority to vocabulary instead of grammar in language learning. As McCarthy (1990) asserts, no matter how well the learners' grammar is and how successfully the sounds of Second language (L2) are pronounced, communication in a second or foreign language cannot be conducted in any meaningful way without words to express various and specific meanings. Vermeer (1992) holds the similar point of view and claims that vocabulary learning is critical for understanding and being understood and should be given the top priority in language learning. Learners also take vocabulary learning as their main task in learning a L2. It is a common phenomenon that many learners in China take an English dictionary with them instead of a grammar book.

Although the critical role of vocabulary in SLA has been recognized, the instruction of vocabulary has been undervalued by many SLA researchers, and the research in this field has suffered a long-term neglect. More theoretical and experimental studies have been conducted in the fields of acquisition of grammar, phonology and discourse studies. Fortunately, there has been a renewed interest in the research of vocabulary acquisition since the mid-1980s. Since then, more and more studies on L2 vocabulary acquisition from different perspectives have been conducted, and various findings and theoretical proposals have been drawn from these studies. Although abundant research in this area has deepened our understanding of L2 vocabulary acquisition, the incredible growing body of experimental studies in this field makes it difficult to keep abreast with current trends. Hence, the next section will give a brief introduction to the background of L2 vocabulary acquisition research in the hope that it may provide a better illustration of the research trends and unsolved problems in this field.

1.2 Background of L2 vocabulary acquisition research

Since the last two decades, great efforts have been made by SLA researchers to give interpretations of L2 vocabulary acquisition from different perspectives. Various types of studies are conducted to define vocabulary knowledge, construct vocabulary competence framework, generalize distinctive types of word learning strategies, and explore efficient and effective ways of vocabulary instruction and acquisition (Verhallen & Schoonen, 1998; Laufer, 1998; Goulden, Nation & Read, 1990; Cohen, 1998; Fraser, 1999; Gu & Johnson, 1996; Nation, 1990; Schmitt, 2000; Webb, 2005). Although researchers have administered a mushrooming amount of experimental studies and theoretical research, it seems difficult to draw congruous conclusions from findings in these studies. On the one hand, there has been a long debate on the effectiveness of intentional instruction and incidental learning on L2 vocabulary acquisition. Some studies in this field are based on the study of First language (L1) vocabulary acquisition in Western countries. Observing the development of vocabulary acquisition by native speakers, some researchers propose that vocabulary learning is just a by-production of reading. It is neither necessary nor practical to learn most of the words through intentional instruction and learning in class. However, recent studies have indicated the insufficiency and ineffectiveness of simply acquiring L2 vocabulary through incidental learning (Parry, 1997; Schmitt, 1998; Wesche & Paribakht, 1996; Zimmerman, 1997; Nation, 2001). On the other hand, the concept of vocabulary knowledge varies over time. The understanding of acquisition of vocabulary knowledge in previous studies is confined to learning the superficial meaning of a word and increasing the vocabulary size. Later research in vocabulary knowledge has indicated that complete word knowledge involves multiple facets of knowledge. According to Nation's (1990) definition of word knowledge, it consists of four levels (form, position, function and meaning), with each level subdivided into two aspects. It takes time and enough exposure to acquire dimensional aspects of word knowledge receptively and productively (Nation, 2001).

Findings from various experimental studies provide more data for hypotheses testing and deepen our understanding of L2 vocabulary acquisition. However, through an in-depth observation of previous studies in L2 vocabulary acquisition, it can be found that most of the studies stay at a relatively superficial level by investigating the different effects of pedagogical methods on vocabulary learning (such as incidental learning with dictionary consulting or extensive reading plus vocabulary practice) or on promoting one or two specific aspects of word knowledge by using some learning strategies (e.g. imaginary strategy for word meaning learning). Among those empirical studies, few have presented in-depth interpretations of the reasons why one instruction method outperforms the other. There still lacks a systematic theoretical framework which can give a comprehensive and thorough illustration of the L2 vocabulary acquisition process.

In recent studies in L2 vocabulary acquisition, more and more researchers have switched their research interest from refining the pedagogical method to interpreting the vocabulary learning process at an in-depth level based on cognitive theories (Barcroft, 2000; Song, 2008; Kwon, 2006). Many SLA models and hypotheses from a cognitive perspective have been proposed, such as Input Processing Model (VanPatten, 1996), Output Hypothesis (Swain, 1995), and Information Processing Model (Skehan, 1998). Although these cognitive theories have been widely applied to many subfields in SLA research, especially in grammar learning, they have not been widely adopted in L2 vocabulary study. It might be of great benefit to construct a systematic framework of L2 vocabulary knowledge development by exploring the cognitive modes underlying different teaching or learning methods.

1.3 Significance of this book

Although multitudinous theories have been proposed to interpret the L2 vocabulary acquisition from various perspectives, no single theory can offer a comprehensive explanation of all the aspects involved in L2 vocabulary acquisition. This research attempts to give a comprehensive investigation of L2 vocabulary acquisition within the information processing framework. Since input processing and output are regarded as two critical stages in the information processing flow, the roles of input processing and output in L2 vocabulary acquisition will be explored in this book.

Respective effects of different cognitive modes involved in specific learning tasks will be compared for the investigation of input processing in L2 vocabulary acquisition. According to Skehan (1998), the focus for instruction in input processing is to maximize the efficiency of input-to-intake transition. It is believed that two cognitive modes, the top-down deductive processing and bottom-up inductive processing, are involved in such a transition process. Hence, the learning tasks involving these two types of cognitive modes will be compared to find which one will better enhance the input encoding process. Factors that may affect the in-depth elaboration of input will also be explored in this study.

The relative effects of different types of input enhancement on input processing will also be contrasted in the present study. Several studies have been conducted to compare the effects of sentence-level input and discourse-level input on input elaboration. Findings from some of these studies suggest that sentence-level input is more beneficial for language acquisition (Wong, 2002). This research will explore whether sentence-level input also has better effects on discourse-level input in L2 vocabulary acquisition.

The role of output plays in L2 vocabulary acquisition will also be explored in this research. According to Gass (1997), output is not only the product of information processing, but also plays an active role in language acquisition by providing learners with opportunities to test their hypotheses on the input. Swain's Output Hypothesis presents the roles of output in language learning in general. Hence, the specific roles of output in L2 vocabulary acquisition will be explored in the present study. The possible limitations of output will also be generalized.

Besides the respective investigations into the two variables in L2 vocabulary acquisition, the co-effects of input and output processing will also be examined to obtain an optimal model for L2 vocabulary acquisition.

Acquisition of depth of vocabulary knowledge in multiple facets will be investigated in this study. The concept of depth of vocabulary knowledge was first proposed by Richards in 1976 and developed by Nation (1990) who believes the word knowledge is multi-faceted and categorizes it into four levels. Although the concept of depth of word knowledge has been widely acknowledged, studies conducted on the acquisition of depth of vocabulary knowledge are still far from sufficient, especially in China. The Vocabulary Knowledge Scale (VKS) developed by Paribakht and Wesche (1997) was adopted in the present study to measure depth of vocabulary knowledge. The test instrument used in most of previous experimental studies can only assess one or two aspects of word knowledge. The VKS used in the present study is a self-report type instrument that consists of five categories and can track the increase of depth of word knowledge in various aspects.

In addition, new methods were used for experimental material selection and preparation in this study. To verify the known word coverage rate in experimental materials in this study, a piece of online software program called "Vocabprofile" (Cobb, 2007) was used to check out the frequency of the words in the text. A piece of software called "Wordnet" was also used to provide sufficient information about synonyms, antonyms and authentic sentence-level instances of a word.

Chapter 2 A review of theories and concepts of vocabulary knowledge

2.1 Introduction

In previous studies, L2 vocabulary acquisition usually refers to the increase of one's vocabulary size. However, with the development of research in vocabulary knowledge, it has been widely acknowledged that vocabulary knowledge consists of various aspects of knowledge. Hence, it seems to be unilateral to assess the acquisition of L2 vocabulary by the increase of vocabulary size. Many other instruments have been developed to assess different aspects of word knowledge. Meanwhile, some researchers propose the concept of lexical competence, which includes more comprehensive dimensions of word acquisition. This chapter will give a brief review of the categorization of vocabulary knowledge and its corresponding assessing instruments. Models of lexical competence proposed by several researchers will also be discussed in this chapter.

2.2 Research on breadth and depth of vocabulary knowledge

Breadth and depth, which are terms in vocabulary research, have appeared in the literature since the early twentieth century. Among various definitions of and distinctions between these two terms, the definition given by Anderson & Freebody (1981: 92-93) in their comments on vocabulary knowledge is a very influential one. They suggest that vocabulary knowledge consists of two dimensions in terms of quantitative and qualitative aspects. The first dimension is the number of words of which the person can tell at least some significant aspects of the meaning. And the second dimension is the quality or "depth" of understanding.

2.2.1 Breadth of vocabulary knowledge

2.2.1.1 Defining breadth of vocabulary knowledge

Breadth of vocabulary knowledge refers to the vocabulary size or number of words a speaker or learner can provide with meaning or other superficial knowledge. It had been regarded as a vital index of vocabulary competence or even language proficiency before depth of vocabulary knowledge was widely acknowledged. Previous studies on breadth of vocabulary knowledge mainly focus on: 1) Measuring the vocabulary size of various types of speakers (native/non-native) or L2 learners (English major/ non-English major) (Goulden et al., 1990; Hazenberg & Hulstijn, 1996; Laufer, 1992; Zhou & Wen, 2000), 2) assessing the correlation between the vocabulary size and reading or writing competency (Laufer, 1989; Li, 2004), and 3) comparing different effects of various pedagogical techniques or learning strategies on vocabulary gains (Gu & Johnson, 1996).

2.2.1.2 Assessing breadth of vocabulary knowledge

The design of the vocabulary size test consists of two phases: Screening sample words from the dictionary and determining the test mode. Words in the tests of vocabulary size for L2 learners are mainly the high-frequency words that they are most likely to encounter in their use of the language. Read (2000) generalizes four test formats commonly used: 1) multiple-choice items of various kinds, 2) matching of words with synonyms or definitions;

3) supplying an L1 equivalent for each L2 target word, and 4) the checklist (or yes-no) test, in which the test-taker simply identifies whether he or she knows the word.

The four vocabulary size test formats have been widely adopted to measure the progress in vocabulary learning. However, each of them has drawbacks which need to be compensated. The multiple-choice test is too time-consuming, for the words are usually contextualized in a sentence or paragraph, which requires more time to read. Moreover, the test-takers' performance is probably dependent on the choice of distractors. The checklist test format also involves the probability of guessing or false recognition from the test takers, and the result reported by the test-takers is too subjective. Among these test formats, a widely accepted one is the Vocabulary Levels Test (VLT), which was first devised by Paul Nation in 1980 and revised several times in the following decades. The test consists of five levels of word frequency in English, which are the first 2000 words level, the 3000 words level, the 5000 words level, the university word level (beyond 5000 words) and the 10000 words level. According to Nation (1990), the first 2000- and 3000-word levels contain the high-frequency words that promise learners to read the unsimplified texts. Although the test format is word-definition matching, the definitions rather than the words are the test items that need to be matched with corresponding words. The sample of the test format is shown as follows:

1. apply
2. elect ______ choose by voting
3. jump ______ become like water
4. manufacture ______ make
5. melt
6. threaten

This type of vocabulary size test format requires less reading and can be taken in a short time. Meanwhile, the words for option are quite different from each other in their semantic senses to decrease the possibility of guessing. For these merits, the VLT is now a commonly accepted test instrument by many researchers in their vocabulary acquisition studies.

Although the vocabulary size tests can present an overview of the test takers' vocabulary level, it is confined to testing the superficial meaning of the target words. It tends to be too simplified to test a target word on its meaning and may ignore other aspects of knowledge concerning that word, such as its synonyms, collocations and grammatical features. Therefore, researchers have turned their attention to the study of depth of word knowledge.

2.2.2 Research on depth of word knowledge

It is widely acknowledged that the acquisition of depth of vocabulary knowledge entails more than just providing a given L2 word with its L1 equivalence or an L2 synonym. Nevertheless, the simple dichotomy is far from being a comprehensive and satisfying concept to guide research and assessments on L2 vocabulary knowledge. Many researchers tend to develop and operationalize the concept of depth of vocabulary knowledge (Richards, 1976; Nation, 1990, Hulstijn, 2001; Wolter, 2001) from different perspectives. These concepts and assumptions on the definition of depth of vocabulary knowledge can be generalized into three types: 1) The continuum-based definition, 2) the dimensional-based definition, and 3) the mental-based definition (Cui, 2008).

2.2.2.1 Continuum-based depth of word knowledge

2.2.2.1.1 Defining continuum-based word knowledge

Some researchers claim that the acquisition of depth of vocabulary knowledge follows a continuum, which starts with a limited, vague idea of a word and ends with a more elaborated, precise knowledge of the word (Faerch et al., 1984; Palmberg, 1987; Henriksen, 1999). Faerch, Haastrub and Phillipson (1984) suggest that at the first phase of the development flow of depth of vocabulary knowledge, learners just have a shallow familiarity with the word form, and at the end of the flow they can use the word correctly in free production (Cui, 2006). Slightly different from Faerch et al.'s proposal, Parmberg (1987) adds two components to the development continuum, namely, receptive knowledge and productive knowledge. This dichotomy concept of the developmental state of word knowledge has been widely accepted and detailed by many researchers (Nation, 1990; Henriksen, 1999). According to Nation (1990), acquisition of receptive word knowledge refers to that learners being able to recognize a word when it is heard or seen, while productive word knowledge requires learners to use the word appropriately in speaking and writing. The receptive words and productive words are also termed as passive words and active words respectively. Laufer and Paribakht (1998) further divide the active words into two categories, the controlled active words which can be used by the impulse of certain task demands, and the free active words used correctly and automatically with the least effort.

Numerous studies have been done on the acquisition of receptive knowledge and productive knowledge (Aitchison, 1987; Clark, 1993; Laufer, 1998; Laufer & Paribakht, 1998; Waring, 1999; Webb, 2005). It has been commonly accepted that the receptive vocabulary is much larger than the productive vocabulary, and that the reception of a word always precedes the production.

However, there still lacks a clear-cut boundary between receptive and productive knowledge. It's difficult to define at what exact point receptive knowledge can be converted into productive knowledge. Melka (1997) has done a thorough study on the receptive and productive aspects of word knowledge. He proposes that knowing a word is not an all-or-nothing proportion. The previous studies which are mainly based on the dichotomy result in disparate assessment of receptive and productive vocabulary and ignore the continuity between the two dimensions. Such disparate research fails to give a precise description of the distance between the two poles. Therefore, Melka (1997) suggests a "non-dichotomy" continuum that views the vocabulary acquisition as an incremental process. In a learning process, many words are only partially known without a full mastery of some lexical aspects such as collocational or functional facets (Schmitt & McCarty, 1997). Some aspects of a word may be acquired productively when other aspects are still at the receptive level. Read (2004) suggests that the definitions of receptive and productive word knowledge seem to be too vague, and there is a lack of specific criteria to assess the two aspects of word knowledge. He believes that the variability in the semantic characteristics of words makes defining a criterion level of precision complicated and impossible. Many high-frequency words are polysemous and have inherently vague meanings. Hence even adult native speakers may just identify in which contexts or registers the words are used but fail to give meaning to those words.

2.2.2.1.2 Assessment of continuum-based word knowledge

Paribakht and Wesche (1993; 1996) believe that the precision of meaning tends to take depth of vocabulary knowledge as a continuum rather than a fixed standard. Hence, they develop an assessing instrument called the VKS test to assess depth of vocabulary knowledge gained by learners through reading. It is a general instrument that provides a test frame and can be used to assess any target words (Read, 2000). It consists of an elicitation scale and a scoring scale. The elicitation scale (see Figure 2-1) presented to test-takers is composed of five self-report categories or steps ordered in the sequence of depth of word knowledge involved in each category.

Impair

I. I don't remember having seen this word before.

II. I have seen this word before, but I don't know what it means.

III. I have seen this word before, and I think it means ______________ (synonyms or translations)

IV. I know this word. It means____________. (synonyms or translations)

V. I can use this word in a sentence:_________(Write a sentence)
(If you do this section, please also do IV.)

Figure 2-1 The VKS elicitation scale: Self-report categories (Paribakht & Wesche, 1997:180)

The scoring scale (see Figure 2-2) translates the test-taker's responses to each word into test scores. Categories I and II responses are credited with scores of 1 and 2 respectively. Wrong responses in Categories III, IV, or V will also be credited with a score of 2. The test-takers can get a score of 3 by providing an appropriate synonym or translation in Categories III or IV. A score of 4 is given if the meaning of the target word fits the sentence context appropriately but is used in a grammatically incorrect way, such as a wrong inflectional or derived form. A score of 5 will be awarded if the word is used both semantically and grammatically correct.

Self- report categories	Possible scores	Meaning of scores
I.	1	The word is not familiar at all.
II.	2	The word is familiar but its meaning is not known.
III.	3	A correct synonym or translation is given.
IV.	4	The word is used with semantic appropriateness in a sentence.
V.	5	The word is used with semantic appropriateness and grammatically accuracy in a sentence.

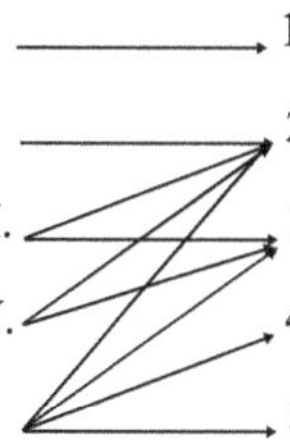

Figure 2-2 The VKS scoring categories (Paribakht and Wesche, 1997: 181)

The VKS has been proven to have high reliability (r=0.89) and validity (r=0.97) in Wesche and Paribakht's (1996) study. The ordered steps show the depth of word knowledge acquisition, from shallow to deep degree, and from recognizing the form of a word in isolation to using it in context which involves comprehensive knowledge (semantic and syntactic knowledge) about the word. As Wesche and Paribakht (1996) claim: "Its purpose is not to estimate the general vocabulary knowledge, but rather to track the early development of specific words in an instructional or experimental situations."

2.2.2.2 Dimensional-based depth of word knowledge

2.2.2.2.1 Defining dimensional-based word knowledge

Definition of depth of word knowledge from a dimensional perspective views that word knowledge consists of various aspects of knowledge which one needs to acquire. The initial definition which can be taken as being dimensional-based appears in Cronbach's article (1942) on vocabulary testing. In this article, he proposes five types of behavior involved in understanding a word: 1) generalization, which refers to the ability to define a word; 2) application, which means using it in contexts appropriately; 3) breadth of meaning, indicating the ability to recall different meanings of a word; 4) precision of meaning, referring to using a word appropriately in various contexts or registers; and 5) availability, which refers to the ability to use a word productively. This definition includes both the meaning aspect of word knowledge and the levels of accessibility to the knowledge. However, many other aspects (such as morphological, syntactical, and formed) are not included in Cronbach's framework. It has been commonly acknowledged that Richards (1976) is the first researcher who has listed relatively comprehensive aspects of word knowledge and proposed the multiple-faceted concept. He assumes that knowing a word includes knowing the frequency, function, register, meaning, collocation, association and grammatical features of the word. He also claims that the word knowledge of native speakers would keep expanding in adult life, as opposed to the relative stability of their grammatical competence. Richards' assumption on vocabulary knowledge seems to be very comprehensive, including more aspects which were neglected in previous studies, such as the frequency, register and grammatical features. However, the generalization by Richards is not flawless, and it misses the spoken and written aspects of a word. Moreover, it seems that the frequency aspect is more important than the associated meaning in his list. Meara (1996) argues that this way of ordering seems to be odd.

Based on Richards' assumptions on word knowledge, Nation (1990) categorizes word knowledge into four levels and each level is further subdivided into two facets. The receptive/productive components are also added to his framework. The four levels are form (spoken/written), position (grammatical patterns/collocations), function (frequency/appropriateness), and meaning (concept/associations), each of which is described in terms of receptive and productive knowledge (see Table 2-1).

Table 2-1 Knowing a word (Nation, 1990: 31)

Form			
	Spoken form	R	What does the sound like?
		P	How is the word pronounced?
	Written form	R	What does the word look like?
		P	How is the word written and spelled?
Position			
	Grammatical patterns	R	In what patterns does the word occur?
		P	In what patterns must we use the word?
Collocations		R	What words or types of words can be expected before or after the word?
		P	What words or types of words must we use with this word?

Continued

Function		
Frequency	R	How common is the word?
	P	How often should we expect to meet this word?
Appropriateness	R	Where would we expect to meet this word?
	P	Where can this word be used?
Meaning		
Concept	R	What does the word mean?
	P	What word should be used to express this meaning?
Associations	R	What other words does this word make us think of?
	P	What other words could we use instead of this one?

Hulstijn (2001) proposes a similar multi-faceted definition and suggests that a lexical entry should contain semantic, pragmatic, stylistic, collocational, syntactic, categorical, morphological, articulatory and orthographic features.

The depth of vocabulary knowledge framework developed by Richards (1976), Nation (1990) and Hulstijn (2001) provide detailed native-like word knowledge. However, the comprehensive property of this framework is criticized as being too idealized and unrealistic. Even native speakers cannot master all aspects of knowledge for every word they know. In most cases, they master only some facets of the knowledge of a familiar word. Schmitt and McCarthy (1997) indicate that it is impossible to design a test which can assess all aspects of the word knowledge. However, recent research has begun to make an attempt to design a battery of tests of word knowledge based on Nation's (1990) framework. This measure instrument will be further discussed in the next section.

2.2.2.2.2 Assessment of the multidimensional-based vocabulary knowledge

Assessment based on the multidimensional framework is more

complicated and involves various tests to assess different aspects of word knowledge. Although it seems to be very difficult to construct a test to assess every aspect of depth of word knowledge, many researchers have tried to incorporate as many aspects as possible to gain a more comprehensive understanding of learners' development of depth of vocabulary knowledge on various facets (Webb, 2005, 2007; Sun, 2006; Liu, 2006; Bai, 2002).

Among these attempts of assessing multiple facets of vocabulary knowledge, Webb's (2005, 2007) design is the most comprehensive one, which consists of a battery of tests assessing the meaning, form and position levels of vocabulary knowledge both in receptive and productive aspects. Only the spoken form on the form level and the function level are not incorporated in his test instruments. The productive knowledge of written form and meaning, grammatical function is tested by dictation, translation and sentence construction respectively. The productive knowledge of syntax and association is assessed by producing the syntagmatic or semantic associates for the prompt words respectively. The receptive knowledge of the meaning, form, and position levels is measured by using multiple choices tests respectively. This analytic test mode which assesses multiple dimensions of depth of vocabulary knowledge by using a battery of tests does provide the researchers with a more comprehensive and deeper understanding of the development of depth of vocabulary knowledge.

However, it should be noted that this type of dimensional-based test instrument still has some drawbacks. First, the multiple choice test format for receptive knowledge assessment increases the difficulty in the design of the test items to assure the validity and reliability of the test instrument. The target words used in Webb's study are nonsensical words rather than authentic words, which makes the design of the test instrument much easier than the ordinary test design, since the distractors in the multiple-choice test items which are also nonsensical words would eliminate the possibility of guessing as an interfering variable. However, this type of target words test method cannot be widely generalized in other tests in which the authentic words should be assessed. It's difficult to ensure the validity and reliability of the tests. Second, the design and administration of such a long battery of tests for each word seem to be too time-consuming. Since the entire series of multiple dimensional-based tests consist of 10 subtests for each target word, including various types of test formats, it is a big challenge for a test designer to design such a huge set of tests for many target words. It also takes too much time to finish the assessment for the test takers. They will lose the patience to accomplish all the subtests. Third, the function level of depth of vocabulary knowledge is not included in this instrument.

In summary, Webb's (2005) multiple dimensional-based test design is the first attempt to give a comprehensive assessment of depth of vocabulary knowledge including both receptive and productive word knowledge according to Nation's (1990) categorization. The battery of tests gives a thorough probe into the development of vocabulary knowledge on various dimensions. However, there still exist some deficiencies to be perfected.

2.2.2.3 Mental-lexical-based depth of word knowledge

2.2.2.3.1 Defining mental-lexical-based word knowledge

Different from studies conducted from dichotomy continuum or multi-dimensional perspectives, some researchers find the correlation between depth of word knowledge and the representation of one's mental lexicon (Schmitt, 1998; Wolter, 2001). Researchers investigate the development of depth of word knowledge by eliciting word associations to probe into the mental state of subjects. Wolter (2001) conducts an experimental study in which the different word association types between children and adults and between native and non-native language learners were contrasted to find the change of mental representations of a word at different word knowledge development stages. According to his findings in this study, Wolter (2001) proposes depth of Individual Word Knowledge (DIWK) Model. In this model, depth of word knowledge is determined by the word association types given by the subjects when they encounter a word and are asked to give an associated word coming first to their mind. Three types of word association responses are generalized in this model: 1) the clang responses, 2) the syntagmatic responses, and 3) the paradigmatic responses. He notes that different association types reflect different word knowledge depth. Children often give clang responses which have similar pronunciation but no semantic association with the prompt word. With their development of vocabulary knowledge and language proficiency, they will be more likely to give syntagmatic responses which can collocate with prompt words in a sentence. For the adult native speakers, most of their responses are paradigmatic types which belong to the same semantic category as the prompt word. The contrast of word association types between native and non-native speakers indicates that L2 learners also follow the changing flow of the word association types.

Through a closer observation of the DIWK model, it can be found that this model has a similarity with Nation's (1990) dimensional-based categorization of the word knowledge. Three lexical features mentioned in Nation's categorization of depth of word knowledge can be generalized in the DIWK model: 1) Clang responses, related to the acquisition of spoken form in Nation's definition, 2) syntagmatic responses, coinciding with collocation in Nation's position aspect, and 3) paradigmatic responses, similar to the semantic association in Nation's meaning aspect.

Although these lexical features appear in two definitions, they are studied from quite different perspectives. In Nation's word knowledge framework, all these three lexical features are paralleled with the same weight of importance in knowing a word; while in the DIWK model, three word association types are assigned different weight of importance as indexes of different lexical development stages. Moreover, the DIWK model does take other lexical aspects such as functional and grammatical features into consideration.

2.2.2.3.2 Assessment on the mental-lexicon-based word knowledge

Due to the various drawbacks discussed in the previous section, many researchers have given up the ambitious attempt to test all aspects of word knowledge and based their design of the depth of lexical knowledge test on the DIWK model (Qian & Schedl, 2004; Read, 2000). Read (2000) develops a word-association task which requires learners to select responses or associates words semantically related to the prompt words. The test format is as follows:

edit

arithmetic	film		pole
publishing revise	risk	surface	text

In the design of this test format, the key factor is to set the standard of selection of the associates. Read (2000) identifies three types of associates: 1) Synonyms (*edit–revise*), 2) collocations (*edit–film*), and 3) analytic words which are the components in the semantic analysis of the prompt word and consist part of the definition (*edit–publishing*). However, the reliability of the test format may be interfered by the possibility of guessing, and it increases the difficulty in choosing appropriate words as distractors in the course of test design. Moreover, this test format design is only confined to assessing adjectives. The reliability and validity of this test instrument for assessing nouns or verbs are still in question and few studies have been conducted in this field.

Taking the high requirement for test responses design in the multiple-choice format into consideration, other researchers propose the open-type test format which asks the learners themselves to provide the associates for the prompt words (Wolter, 2002; Schmitt, 1998; Cui, 2006). The test format can be illustrated as follows:

surging ______________ _______ _______

Answers provided by test-takers are contrasted with a norm list in which different types of word associations of prompt words provided by native speakers are listed and assigned different weights. Responses with high frequency in the norm list will be assigned greater weight than the low frequency responses. This test format can provide information on the degree of similarity between test-takers' word association types and the native speakers'. However, there still lacks a sound standard for establishing the norm list. Moreover, the reliability of weighing responses according to their frequency in the norm list is still questioned.

In summary, there are mainly three types of definitions of depth of vocabulary knowledge: 1) The continuum-based definition, 2) the dimensional-based definition, and 3) the mental-based definition. These three types of definitions view depth of vocabulary knowledge from various perspectives, but it should also be noted that there exist some parallels or overlaps among them to some extent. For instance, both the continuum-based and dimensional-based definitions involve the concepts of receptive knowledge and productive knowledge. Three word association types in the mental-based definition can find their correspondence in the dimensional-based definition. The different testing modes corresponding to the three types of definitions also have their respective merits and drawbacks. Researchers can use one or two of them simultaneously according to their own needs to conduct a comprehensive investigation into the acquisition and development of depth of word knowledge.

2.3 Theories on lexical competence

The previous sections have reviewed various definitions of the qualitative and quantitative aspects of word knowledge respectively. These definitions view word knowledge from different perspectives and focus on different lexical features or facets. However, vocabulary acquisition is a complex process and involves many aspects. Different from the previous views which seem to be word-centered and emphasize only one or two aspects of word knowledge, other researchers propose the concept of lexical competence, which regards vocabulary acquisition as a complex process comprising many aspects (Chapelle, 1994, 1998; Meara, 1996; Zhang & Wu, 2003). Three lexical competence frameworks will be reviewed in the following sections.

2.3.1 Meara's framework

Different from previous studies focusing on the knowledge of lexical features or components of individual words, Meara (1996) proposes a three-dimensional framework of lexical competence. The first dimension is the vocabulary size, which is the same as breadth of word knowledge discussed in previous sections. The second dimension is lexical organization, which is regarded as the richness of a word linkage with other words in one's mental lexicon. The third dimension in his framework is the speed of access, which is used to indicate to what extent a word can be retrieved automatically. It can be found that depth of vocabulary knowledge has not been included in this framework. Meara holds that breadth of vocabulary knowledge is a critical index of one's lexical competency at his early stage of language learning. When a language learner's vocabulary size crosses the threshold of 5000 to 6000 words, the lexical organization or mental lexical network replaces vocabulary size and becomes a more important indicator of lexical competence. Those with a well-structured mental lexicon will give better performance on authentic language tasks than those with less organized vocabulary of the same size. Thus, Meara incorporates the mental lexicon factor into his framework and shifts the study emphasis from the componential features of the word itself to the way of lexical organization in learners' minds. Another important factor proposed by Meara is automaticity, which is regarded as a vital variable affecting the development of receptive and productive capacity in language use.

2.3.2 Henriksen's framework

Henriksen (1999) also proposes a three-dimensional framework of lexical competence: 1) Partial-precise knowledge, 2) depth of knowledge, and 3) receptive-productive knowledge. The partial-precise knowledge dimension suggests that vocabulary learning must experience the process from rough or vague comprehension or categorization of a word to more precision and mastery of finer shades of meaning. This dimension concerns primarily the semantization process of mapping meaning onto form. In contrast with Meara's framework, in which vocabulary size is taken as a vital index of lexical competence, Henriksen encompasses depth of vocabulary knowledge as an important dimension in his framework. The concept of depth of word knowledge in this proposal concerns the quality of learners' vocabulary knowledge and is similar to Nation's (1990) definition, which includes various lexical features of a word. Moreover, Henriksen's depth of knowledge dimension is also associated with mental lexicon network building, which is similar to the lexical organization dimension in Meara's framework. In contrast with the partial-precise knowledge dimension, which emphasizes the semantization process of an individual word, the depth of knowledge dimension is more concerned with creating intentional links between different works. However, Henriksen (1999) also indicates the effect of depth of knowledge development on the progress of partial-precise continuum. She argues that the knowledge of a given word grows in its relationship with other words. As to the receptive-productive knowledge dimension, it is more related to the control or accessibility facet of lexical competence and concerns the levels of access to word knowledge in accomplishing receptive or productive tasks.

2.3.3 Zhang and Wu's framework

Zhang and Wu (2003) develop a lexical competence framework based on the previous theoretical studies and tend to describe the lexical competence from a cognitive perspective. This framework consists of four dimensions: 1) Vocabulary size, 2) depth of vocabulary knowledge, 3) precision of vocabulary use, and 4) automaticity of lexical access.

Compared with the previous two frameworks, which include only one aspect of vocabulary knowledge, the quantitative or qualitative aspect, Zhang and Wu's framework seems to be more comprehensive by incorporating both aspects of word knowledge. The depth of word knowledge dimension in this framework also concerns the development of one's mental lexicon and emphasizes the correlation between the richness of mental lexicon and progress of lexical knowledge of individual words. This notion coincides with Henriksen's proposal. The precision of lexical use is mainly concerned with the functional and semantic aspects of knowledge. It refers to the ability to use a word like a native speaker in various registers without being affected by one's L1 lexical system. The last dimension, the automaticity of lexical access, indicates the developmental flow from controlled to automatic processing in vocabulary retrieval.

Zhang and Wu's framework is not a simple integration of the previous frameworks, but encompasses a mediating variable from a cognitive perspective. They claim that noticing plays a critical role in the development of lexical competence. This proposal has not been mentioned in all the former frameworks which confine their research focus to learning or organization of vocabulary and ignore the cognitive factor with a great effect on the development of lexical competence. The next chapter will present a review of the learning process from a cognitive perspective and will also discuss the role of attention or noticing in L2 vocabulary acquisition.

Chapter 3 Cognitive studies on L2 vocabulary acquisition

3.1 Introduction

The previous section has reviewed the basic concepts and theories on the development of L2 vocabulary knowledge and lexical competence. However, it should be noted that most of these studies focus on what should be acquired or learned in the acquisition process. Although some researchers have incorporated the mental lexicon organization into their frameworks, they are more concerned with the state of lexical representation in the mind in different developmental stages and give little description to the dynamic process of lexicon development from a cognitive perspective. Only Zhang and Wu (2003) encompass noticing as an important cognitive factor affecting lexical acquisition in their lexical competence framework. In fact, many L2 acquisition researchers have realized the important role cognition plays in SLA. They have proposed various cognitive models to interpret the developmental flow of SLA and applied these findings to pedagogical areas to facilitate the L2 acquisition process (Bruner, 1983; Krashen, 1985; Schmidt, 1990; McLaughlin, 1990; VanPatten, 1996, 2003; Gass & Selinker, 2001; Skehan, 1998; Swain, 1995). The following sections will review several of these cognitive models and their applications to L2 acquisition.

3.2 Levels of processing and degree of encoding elaboration

3.2.1 Basic ideas on levels of processing

Craik and Lockhart (1972) propose the processing framework for human memory, which holds that human memory is affected by the levels of information processing. The deeper information is processed or encoded, the longer the retention will maintain. Treisman (1964, 1979) also suggests that perceptual processing can be hierarchical and consists of "levels of analysis". This hierarchy ranges from shallower-level analysis of sensory and surface features to deeper-level analysis of identification of pictures, objects or the meaning of words.

To further investigate the specific levels of the processing framework, Craik and Lockhart (1975) have designed ten different experiments which demand different levels of processing, including both structural and semantic involvement. It is proved in this study that word encoding tasks which require semantic involvement are associated with higher retention levels than tasks which require structural involvement. The findings suggest that it is the nature of encoding that determines learning or memory performance. Studies on dichotic listening (Treisman, 1964, 1979) also prove that deeper analysis of meaning takes more attention than shallower-level analysis of sensory features. Subjects can identify a speaker's voice as male or female with little attention, but fail to catch the meaning of the utterance.

One of the important concepts proposed about levels of processing is to confirm that memory or remembering is processing, which is a dynamic activity of the mind. This idea is quite different from the structural notions of memory traces, which regard memory traces as static entities that need to be searched for, found, and reactivated. Craik and Lockhart (2002) believe that remembering is not a mechanical process which searches and reactivates the information stored in one's mind, but a process which can reflect the qualitative types of initial perception and comprehension. The deeper processing involving meaning processing will lead to higher levels of subsequent remembering.

3.2.2 Modification of the previous notions of levels of processing

Although it reveals the qualitative distinction between the effects of structural and semantic processing on subsequent retention, there are some deficiencies found in some notions of levels of processing (Craik & Lockhart, 1975). Firstly, the stimuli are not always processed along the continuum from structural to semantic processing. It is assumed that although some structural analysis occurs before semantic analysis, a full structural analysis doesn't finish before the semantic analysis.

Lockhart et al. (1975) suggest structural and semantic processing seem to be better viewed as different "domains" of encoding (Sutherland, 1972) rather than a continuum. Therefore, the term "spread" rather than "depth" might be more appropriate to illustrate the different encoding domains involved in information processing. Thus, encoding processing will be better explained in terms of breadth of analysis in each domain rather than a sequential process. Although the modified theory describes different encoding involvement with a more flexible notion, spread or elaboration, instead of in an ordinal position, it still stresses the principal effect of the qualitative nature of encoding operations on retention.

The second deficiency is that the previous notions are too simplified to restrict the depth of analysis to the structural and the semantic level. It seems to be far from adequate to describe information processing only on the nominal levels, such a structural processing level and semantic processing level. The complexity of the encoding context is also an important factor which can affect the retention performance. Differential depth of encoding can only give a description of information processing by using very general terms.

It is found that the stimulus or input entailing complex sentence frames with rich semantic information will require more cognitive elaboration and lead to better retention (Craik et al., 1975). It is suggested that the term elaboration is better in distinguishing different degrees of encoding efforts involved in each encoding domain.

3.2.3 New perspectives on intentional and incidental L2 vocabulary acquisition based on Levels of Processing Model

3.2.3.1 Distinctions between intentional and incidental learning in the operational aspect

Incidental learning is clearly distinguished from intentional learning in experimental studies (Hustijn, 2001). In the operational field, the difference between the two terms lies in testing the target vocabulary with or without forewarning learners before conducting the treatment. In an incidental learning condition, learners will be asked to complete the comprehension tasks while they are reading, while vocabulary acquisition is just regarded as a by-product in the reading comprehension process. In contrast, learners will be clearly informed in an intentional context that they should pay special attention to the target words and are forewarned that there will be a subsequent word retention test after the learning process.

2.2.3.2 Distinctions between the two terms in the psychological aspect

Although the distinction between these two terms is clear-cut in operational terms, it arouses continuous dispute in the psychological field.

Attention engagement is the core index to differentiate incidental learning and intentional learning, and psychologists have a persistent debate on how to define a real incidental learning condition in which no attention is allotted to the target words. McGeoch (1942) holds that it is difficult to prove whether subjects in incidental learning conditions have devoted any attention to the target words or not. Many psychologists gradually accept McGeoch's view and abandon the attempt to distinguish these two notions in terms of attention (Eysenck, 1982). Instead, they put more emphasis on the differences between incidental and intentional learning in terms of instruction treatment and retention measures.

Psychologists' view on the distinction between incidental and intentional learning has changed a lot since Lockhart and Craik proposed their influential notion of depth of processing in 1972. They suggest that processing on the structural or semantic level will lead to different retention performance. Semantic processing will leave a deeper memory trace than structural processing does. They also use the term "elaboration" to differentiate degrees of processing on each depth level. Since then, researchers have shifted their focus from whether attention is engaged in the learning process to how deep the words are processed. They hold a unified view that one's memory performance is mainly determined by the quality of processing activities rather than his/her intention to learn. Many researchers agree that the more elaborate a word is processed, the better the word will be learned and retained.

To sum up, from a cognitive perspective, the difference between incidental and intentional learning lies in the quality and frequency of information processing and no longer reflects a principal theoretical distinction. The critical determiner of successful vocabulary learning and retention is the depth and degree of elaboration, which can be realized by a variety of task demands and vocabulary exercises.

3.3 Psycholinguistic processes in L2 vocabulary acquisition

Although Craik's Level of Processing theory has differentiated specific levels or degrees of information processing, it mainly focuses on the results of information processing caused by different depth of elaboration and gives no description of the concrete stages involved in the information processing flow. Input, central processing and output are considered to be three critical stages in information processing and have great impact on the language learning process (Skehan, 1998). Various models have been proposed to give interpretation of the roles of different stages playing in the L2 development. The following sections will give a review of different cognitive models and their applications to L2 vocabulary acquisition.

3.3.1 Input and L2 vocabulary acquisition

Many SLA researchers regard the language development as a flow which starts from input exposure and processing to linguistic output which is also known as language production (VanPatten, 1996, 2003; Gass & Selinker, 2001; Skehan, 1998). The existing models from the information processing perspective mainly focus on exploring the cognitive interpretation of the development of specific stages and conversion process from one stage to another in SLA. Despite the fact that these researchers hold the same view on the general development flow of SLA, their information models differ from each other by assigning different importance to different developmental stages.

3.3.1.1 Krashen's Input Hypothesis

Krashen developed a comprehensive theoretical framework of SLA. In this framework, Krashen proposes the Input Hypothesis which claims that humans acquire language in only one way—by understanding messages, or by receiving comprehensible input (Krashen, 1985). The concept of comprehensible input is illustrated by the formula $i + 1$, where i represents learners' current level of language competence and *1* the next level of competence in the natural order of development. However, Krashen's Input Hypothesis refers to acquisition, not learning. He holds the view that if there is sufficient comprehensible input in which the linguistic items are automatically provided, there is no need to teach linguistic items deliberately since it can be acquired subconsciously with the assistance of the internal language processor—Chomsky's Language Acquisition Device (LAD).

Krashen's Input Hypothesis has a great impact on the pedagogical field in L2 teaching. Immersion program is one of the typical teaching methods which are greatly affected by Krashen's position on comprehensible input. In the immersion program, all the courses are taught in the target language for the purpose that learners can get sufficient exposure to the target language. A longitudinal study on the effectiveness of this method shows that the learners enrolled in the immersion program performed as well as native French students on tests of reading and listening comprehension. However, they failed to show native-like proficiency in speaking and writing skills (Krashen, 1984). Although they could accomplish communicative tasks with high degree of fluency, low rates of accuracy found in their expressions should not be ignored.

Some flaws in Krashen's Input Hypothesis should be noted. Nagy and Anderson (1994) have argued that it is the *comprehended* input rather than the *comprehensible* input that plays a critical role in language learning. In Krashen's Input Hypothesis, input processing seems to depend too much on learners' innate language acquisition device while other cognitive factors are not mentioned in his proposal. Different from Krashen's comprehension-based approach to input, VanPatten (1996) develops the Input Processing Models, which gives more emphases on the cognitive process involved in the conversion of input into intake. The next section will give a thorough introduction to this model in detail.

3.3.1.2 VanPatten's Input Processing Model

Before introducing VanPatten's (1996) Input Processing Model, an illustration of three principles on which input processing is based must be given first.

Principle 1:

Learners process input for meaning before they process it for form.

Principle 2:

For learners who process form that is non-meaningful, e.g. third person–*s*, they must be able to process informational or communicative content at no (or little) cost to attention.

Principle 3:

Learners possess default strategies that assign the role of agent to the first noun (phrase) they encounter in a sentence. (Skehan, 1998, p. 47)

These principles reveal learners' cognitive features in input processing and regard attention as a crucial construct in cognitive psychology. VanPatten (1996) believes that something that is not detected has no chance to be acquired. Although not all the things that are detected can be acquired, attention is the prerequisite for language acquisition. In VanPatten's view, learners are limited-capacity processors with limited attentional resources. They are apt to assign their attention to meaning extracting, which is more useful in accomplishing communicative tasks. Attention could be assigned to the less communicative forms or grammatical features only if the communicative content can be processed with little or no attentional resource. In other words, it is necessary to deliberately draw learners' attention to these linguistic forms or grammatical features, which is termed as "focus on form".

Based on these principles of input processing, VanPatten (1996, 2003) proposes the Information Processing Model which divides the entire course of SLA into three stages. At the first stage (see Figure 3-1), the information is transferred from input into intake by constructing the form-meaning connection. The word "form" in this proposal refers to the formal and grammatical features of the language, such as pronunciation, inflections and functional items like prepositions, articles and pronouns. In addition to the interpretation of form at the syntactic level, it can also be used at the word level to refer to the verbal and written forms of a word (Barcroft, 2000). For example, all words have forms and referents. Regarding the word *girl*, the written form of this word is composed of the letters g-i-r-l. The referent is the meaning of the word, "a young human being who is female". Meaning, then, is interpreted as the referential real-world meaning. A form-meaning connection is made when a learner gets the referential meaning by encoding the form of a linguistic item. When a learner hears *She arrived at the airport in time* and understands *arrived* means the action is in the past, the form-meaning connection is then made. At the next stage, the form-meaning connection, which is also entitled as intake, is stored in the working memory and has the potential to be internalized. Once the intake is internalized, this new linguistic data will be accommodated into the developing linguistic system. This accommodation process will restructure the developing system. This process, however, may be partial or incomplete since some linguistic items or certain aspects of an item fail to be incorporated into the developing system for some reason. At the final stage of the development, the linguistic data that have been accommodated into the developing system may be eventually accessed by the learners as output or production.

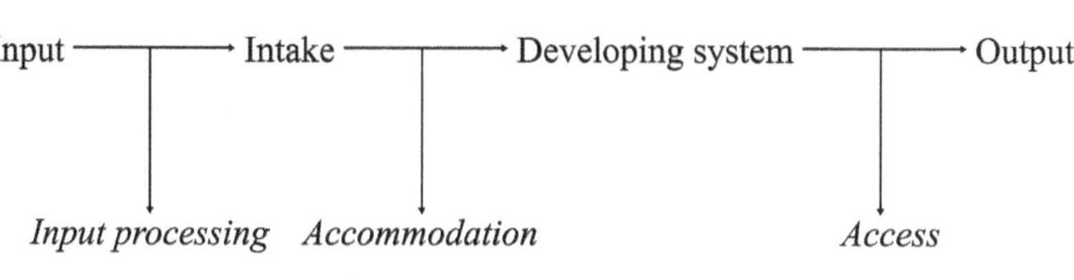

Figure 3-1 Three sets of processes in SLA and use (adapted from Johnson, 2004)

Among the three stages, the conversion from input into intake is believed to be the critical stage for language acquisition in this model. It has been discussed that attention is a crucial prerequisite for acquisition. However, it's far from enough for learners to just notice the linguistic form. In order to make a successful form-meaning connection, learners also need to comprehend the meaning that the form encodes (Wong, 2001). For example, a learner of English may notice the plural maker *–s* in the noun *boys* in the sentence *The boys are very naughty*, but may not understand that *–s* encodes the meaning of plurality. In this case, the learner has noticed the form but has not made a form-meaning connection. With subsequent exposure to and notice of the form, the learner may comprehend the form and make a form-meaning connection. Therefore, attention and comprehension are two factors that affect the conversion of input into intake.

In contrast with Krashen's (1985) Input Hypothesis which highlights meaning-extracting and which takes a comprehension-based approach to input, VanPatten's (1996) Input Processing Model adopts the processing-based approach and stresses more on the role of attention and comprehension in acquisition.

3.3.2 Input and L2 vocabulary acquisition

Krashen's input hypothesis has a great impact on L2 vocabulary acquisition and arouses the debate on the effectiveness of learning words incidentally through extensive reading. By generalizing 144 previous studies on vocabulary learning, Krashen (1989) suggests that incidental vocabulary learning takes place by providing large exposure to comprehensible input through reading. By acknowledging reading is not the only way of vocabulary acquisition, he argues that reading is the most efficient external factor for vocabulary learning if the reading materials are comprehensible and are read with a focus on the message. Learners can expand their vocabulary if they can read for interest and pleasure, even if they do not understand every word in the materials. In contrast with learning words by rote or drill, encoding with meaning exposure in a real communicative context will realize the long-term retention of new words. Krashen (1982) has suggested that learners may develop two systems—an acquired competence and a learned competence. The way of teaching words by presenting decontextualized words results in learned competence, but the acquired competence can only be developed by accessing comprehensible input. This argument is strongly supported by McCarthy (1990) who argues that a word learned in a meaning context can be best assimilated and remembered. Schwartz (1993) also suggests that the language module in the mind can only encode primary linguistic data, and the explicit practice is not usable by the module and can only result in the "learned linguistic knowledge". It is suggested that extensive reading which focuses on a single topic can help learners attain natural repetition of target words or sentence structures. Krashen (1982) believes the comprehensible input gained in reading may lead to progress of the general language competence in both oral and written performance.

Krashen's Input Hypothesis is regarded as one of the most supportive theories for interpreting incidental vocabulary learning (Nagy et al., 1985). The proposition of learning words through reading is mainly based on research into the L1 language acquisition in which children learn vocabulary in their L1. Researchers in this position suggested that vocabulary learning is a by-product of extensive reading. The influential studies in this respect are publications by Nagy and Anderson (1984), Nagy et al. (1985), and Nagy and Herman (1987). They argue that American high school students know 25000–50000 words or even more (Nagy & Anderson, 1984). It is impossible to acquire such a great amount of words solely through the instruction in the class. Instead, the vast majority of words are learned incrementally through repeated encounters in different contexts over time (Nagy, & Anderson, 1984; Nagy et al., 1985; Nagy & Herman, 1987). Many other L1 acquisition studies have proved that learners' vocabulary expands mainly through extensive reading after they break the first-thousand-basic-word threshold (Saragi et al., 1978). Only a small number of words are acquired through direct learning in the classroom.

In Saragi et al.'s (1978) study, they asked the learners to learn new words through reading a novel and finishing reading comprehension tasks. The result showed that considerable words had been acquired with an average of seventy-six percent accuracy in the multiple-choice vocabulary test. It suggests that the learners had picked up about forty-five words incidentally by reading a novel.

Researchers who insist on incidental learning acknowledge that it is still an open question of how incidental learning takes place. It should be noted that the argument of vocabulary acquisition through reading is a default one, which argues that most words are acquired from reading because relatively few words are explicitly taught. Nevertheless, some researchers argue that the growth of vocabulary by learners between the ages of 6 and 16 is not solely the result of reading, but rather owning to a variety of oral and written tasks which force learners to process new words elaborately and repeatedly (Corson, 1997; Hulstijn, 2001). These tasks provide learners with more chances to encode new lexical information and gradually accumulate knowledge of new words. It is the joint effect of exposure frequency and the quality of word encoding that determines the acquisition of new words. Therefore, it seems to be too simple to conclude that extensive reading is the only thing learners need to do to acquire new words.

Based on the review of studies on learning words through reading, it seems that exposing learners to comprehensible input through reading is an ideal way of vocabulary expansion. However, in recent studies, more and more researchers argue that vocabulary learning requires the distribution of attention to both meaning and form (Robinson, 1996; VanPatten, 1996; Izumi, 2003).

In the three input processing principles, VanPatten (1996) suggests that learners process input for meaning before they process it for form, and they prefer processing semantic information to grammatical items. Even when they process the grammatical features of a word such as the word's morphological feature, they prefer encoding "more meaningful" morphology before "less or non-meaningful" ones. When they are provided with the reading materials containing new words, learners will be apt to assign their attention to inferring the meaning of the new words through context to accomplish the comprehension task. They only pay attention to the superficial meaning of the new words in the context and possibly ignore other aspects of knowledge of the words, such as their association, collocation, and grammatical features. For the words that would not affect the comprehension of the text, these features may be totally ignored by the learners while they are reading.

It has been discussed that acquisition of a word does not just mean acquiring the superficial meaning of the word but involves many aspects of lexical knowledge. As Craik (1975) has suggested, encoding the word on only one lexical aspect will not lead to long-term retention. A better retention of a word can be achieved by encoding the word on various lexical aspects elaborately. Yet, the pure comprehensible input through reading is more meaning-extracting oriented and tends to induce learners to ignore other aspects of lexical knowledge. It can be inferred that the solely comprehensible input is far from sufficient for vocabulary learning at the input processing stage. VanPatten (1996) suggests that learners' attention should be drawn to the formal features of the linguistic items. As to learning a word, the formal features are not just confined to the oral and written forms of the word, but also involve many other lexical aspects such as collocation, grammatical features and morphological features.

3.3.2.1 Cognitive modes involved in input processing

There exist two types of processing or reasoning modes for input processing: Inductive processing and deductive processing. In the case of inductive processing, one learns something by perceiving a number of specific exemplars and induces a general rule or principle that governs the specific instances or represents the features of these specific instances. In contrast, deductive reasoning runs in the opposite direction. In the case of deductive reasoning, learners are first exposed to a general rule or principle, and specific instances demonstrating the application of the rule are then presented. These two cognitive modes are applied to L2 learning and teaching field and lead to the development of different teaching and learning approaches. The traditional methods, such as the Grammar-Translation method or intentional method, greatly focus on the use of deductive reasoning in language teaching and learning. In these rule-based approaches, learners are primarily provided with explicit instruction on the target grammatical rules or features of a target linguistic item, and then asked to further elaborate the grammatical rules or linguistic items through instances encoding. This type of rule-based approach is more teacher-centered and gets theoretical support from the behaviorism, which regards learning as a stimulus-response process. Learners are considered as mechanical knowledge receivers who passively learn knowledge through explicit instructions and drills.

However, teachers using exemplar-based inductive approaches do not instruct the rules explicitly but ask learners to infer or generalize the target rules from the given instances on their own. The incidental learning which insists natural and untutored learning, as well as L1 learning, involves a largely inductive process. In these inductive approaches, learners play a critical role in the learning process. The effectiveness of the inductive approach is supported by the constructivists (Piaget, 1972; Vygotsky, 1978; Bruner, 1983) who argue that learning is an active knowledge construction process which greatly depends on learners' own mental processing rather than on the information transmission from teachers. Piaget (1972), the founding figure of constructivism, holds that learning is not a mechanical memorizing process but involves a complex and dynamic interplay in which the mind encodes the input to fit it into the existing knowledge system or reversely restructures the existing system to accommodate the new concepts. Bruner (1983), another constructivist, holds the same idea as Piaget, and further proposes that learning is a learner-centered process in which learners select and encode the information, and make hypotheses from the information and accommodate the new concept into their existing system through reflecting and abstraction.

3.3.2.2 Roles of input in L2 vocabulary acquisition

As an important factor for language development at the first stage, input provides learners with primary linguistic materials for encoding and processing. Researchers have generalized several features of input in language learning. Two features which are more related to vocabulary acquisition will be introduced in the next two sections.

3.3.2.2.1 High frequency of word exposure

Studies investigating the effect of reading on vocabulary acquisition have found that both L1 and L2 learners may incidentally gain knowledge of meaning and form through reading (Nagy et al., 1985; Dupuy & Krashen, 1993; Hulstijn, 1992). The main point of these studies is that incidental vocabulary learning is a gradual process in which gains are made incrementally with repeated encounters. It is also suggested that repetition of words in reading texts can facilitate lexical inference, and it has been taken as a principle for constructing graded reading materials since an adequate amount of reading materials may provide learners with more opportunities to encounter a target word in different contexts.

This position has been supported by empirical evidence from studies in both L1 and L2 learning contexts. An L1 study conducted by Jenkins et al. (1984) shows that vocabulary gains increase as the number of times learners meet words in context increases. Learners who meet words 10 times produce superior scores to those who meet words only twice.

Rott (2004) conducted a study to investigate whether intermediate learners can acquire and retain new words incidentally through reading. In his study, learners in three groups were exposed to new words two, four, or six times respectively during reading. The result indicates that learners with six encounters of new words during reading performed best in the vocabulary acquisition test.

Similar studies have also been done in China (Shu, 2006). Shu (2006) has conducted a study to investigate the effects of amount of exposure on L2 vocabulary learning. According to the result in this study, she concludes that a word will be well-learned on both receptive and productive aspects when it is exposed more than eight times. She also suggests that part of speech does not influence vocabulary gains when the words are exposed to learners with the same frequency in the text. Nevertheless, the result indicates that there is no obvious correlation between the contextual richness and vocabulary acquisition.

The studies reviewed above all show a positive correlation between the frequency of exposure and L2 vocabulary acquisition. It seems that a word can be successfully learned on both receptive and productive knowledge when it is exposed to learners at least 6 times. However, not all the studies give positive evidence of the crucial relationship between the frequency of word exposure and L2 vocabulary acquisition. Some researchers conclude from their studies that there is no fixed number of repetitions that will ensure learning. In fact, contextual richness has a very strong influence on the number of word exposure needed to gain knowledge of a target word (Nation & Wang, 1999; Webb, 2007). Contextual richness, another important variable affecting L2 vocabulary acquisition, will be discussed in the next section.

3.3.2.2.2 Contextual richness

Many researchers have acknowledged that inferring the meanings of unfamiliar words in contexts is an important way of vocabulary learning (Carton, 1971; Huckin & Bloch, 1993; Li, 2004; Schouten-van Parreren, 1996; Webb, 2007). Hence, the contextual richness is of vital importance to word inference. The more informative a context is, the easier it is for a learner to infer the meaning of an unfamiliar word. According to the schema theory, word inference seems to be a process of inferring unknown words by means of using relevant schemata (Widdowson, 1983). Schemata can be regarded as references which provide a basis for information predication and organization in the long-term memory. Two features of an informative context are generalized. Firstly, the context must be perceptually and conceptually familiar to the learner. Secondly, it must contain the information available for the learner to find the relevant schemata to identify unfamiliar words which appear in the context.

Schouten-van Parreren (1996) has made a critical comment on the traditional decontextualized word list learning method. This comment can also give cogent support to the positive effect of context on L2 vocabulary learning from another perspective. Schouten-van Parreren (1996) points out that the words presented in isolation from contexts provide no "cognitive hold" for them in learners' memory and will be forgotten very quickly. These decontextualized words fail to present a psychological reality and cannot evoke learners' emotional learning involvement, which is critical for long-term acquisition.

Gass (1999) has categorized various types of contexts which can facilitate inference of unfamiliar word meaning. She points out that the meaning of an unknown word can be inferred with the assistance of the lexical, grammatical, verbal, situational, and cultural contexts. Learners can also attain the collocational meaning of words with the help of lexical context clues and learn the grammatical features or structures of a word through the grammatical context. The verbal and situational contexts and background knowledge can provide learners with sufficient contextual cues to infer the meaning of an unknown word.

Many empirical studies in this field also present positive evidence for the effect of contextual richness on L2 vocabulary learning (Li, 2004; Nation & Wang, 1999; Webb, 2007). Li (1988) conducted an empirical study to compare the effects of contextual adequacy on word inference and retention in both reading and listening contexts. The results support the position that contextual richness affects inference and retention of unknown words in the context. Participants who received cue-adequate sentences reported greater ease in word inference than those who received cue-inadequate sentences. It is also found that there is a positive correlation between word inference and word retention. Learners who performed better word inference with the assistance of adequate contextual cues scored significantly higher in word retention.

3.3.3 Input enhancement approach to L2 vocabulary acquisition

As discussed above, frequency and contextual richness are two variables affecting the effectiveness of meaning inference and retention of an unknown word. A great deal of research in this field has also given supportive evidence for this position. However, it's important to note that the real incidental learning context cannot consistently provide learners with reading materials containing frequent repetitions and adequate contextual cues. These variables, such as the number of unknown words, repetition frequency, and the level of information in the context, will vary from text to text. Moreover, learners in L2 learning context need to learn at a faster rate than the "natural" rate of L1 acquisition. The lack of sufficient word repetitions and adequate contextual cues in reading materials make the incidental L2 vocabulary learning impossible. It seems to be too time-consuming for a learner to learn a word by reading a great number of reading materials through a long period of time. It is also possible that a learner has forgotten a target word when he or she encounters it again after a long time interval. The low frequency of word repetition cannot effectively attract learners' attention to the target word form and make form-meaning connections to convert the input into intake.

3.3.3.1 Input flood

Some pedagogical techniques have been developed to compensate for the deficiency of incidental learning context. One of these techniques is called input flood, which aims to draw learners' attention to a target linguistic item by flooding the input with many exemplars of the linguistic item. The frequent and dense input may direct learners' attention to the target linguistic item and make more elaborated encoding on it.

The input flood can be carried out by taking both written and oral input. In the written mode, input can be modified by means of embedding many exemplars of the target linguistic item into the reading materials. For instance, an article or a story can be modified so that the target linguistic item can appear in this reading material over and over again. Many advantages have been found in the input flood method. One of the main advantages is that a great deal of meaning-bearing input is provided in the learning materials.

A lot of studies have investigated the effect of input flood on language learning (Trahey & White, 1993; Williams, 1999). One of the first empirical studies on input flood was conducted by Trahey and White (1993). They investigated the effectiveness of input flood in teaching young French-speaking ESL learners adverb placement in English. Learners were exposed to input flooded with hundreds of instances of English adverbs over a two-week period. No explicit instruction was given to teach the rules for adverb placement, and no error correction was provided. Adverbs were simply embedded in the reading materials. The results indicate that the input flood is effective in facilitating the acquisition of adverb placement. However, it seems to be ineffective in helping learners acknowledge which adverb placement positions are not possible in English.

As indicated in VanPatten's (1996) input principles, learners are apt to process input for meaning before they process it for form. The meaning-bearing input provides learners with authentic linguistic contexts in the process of target linguistic item encoding. The second advantage of input flood is that it does not disrupt the flow of communication and keeps learners' attention to the meaningful task (Doughty & Williams, 1998). Another advantage of input flood is that no special teaching or explaining is needed. All the instructor needs to do is to saturate the reading materials with the target linguistic items (Wong, 2005). It can be considered as a type of implicit way to draw learners' attention to the linguistic form by means of input flood. However, it's important to note that the feature of implicit input flood provision may increase the difficulty for instructors to know whether learners have noticed the target form and whether they are actually learning anything through the input flood. Moreover, this type of input enhancement technique has its limitations in the application area. It can only be applied easily to grammatical items learning by embedding the target form into reading materials without changing the meaning of the texts, while it seems to be rather difficult to embed a target word frequently in a reading material without affecting the authenticity of the text.

3.3.3.2 Textual enhancement

As discussed in the previous section, the input flood technique has a fatal deficiency: it is difficult to verify whether learners have noticed the target form flooded in the modified input. Another input enhancement technique, textual enhancement, which can compensate for this deficiency, will be introduced in this section. In contrast with input flood, the textual enhancement technique draws learners' attention to linguistic items in a more explicit way by using typographical cues such as bolding and italics. Here is an example:

> I **must** get more sleep. If not, I **may** not wake up for work. I **may** have to drink lots of coffee and then I **may** be nervous all day. It **must** be close to midnight right now. I **must** stop staying up so late at night. (Wong, 2005, p. 68)

A target linguistic item can also be modified by other types of typographical manipulations such as underlying or altering the font, character size or style of the target form. The essential idea behind this technique is to make a certain written item which is easily ignored by learners more salient.

Although an array of studies has been conducted to verify the effect of textual enhancement on SLA (Shook, 1994; Alanen, 1995; Overstreet, 1998;

Wong, 2002), no consistent conclusion can be drawn from these studies. In Alanen's (1995) study, he compared the relative effects of four learning types (rules instruction plus textual enhancement, rules only, textual enhancement only, text only without rules instruction and textual enhancement) on grammatical morphemes learning. The results show that textual enhancement does help learners notice the target form. But it also shows that learners receiving only rules instruction perform better in the production test than learners receiving textual enhancement only. Alanen concludes from these findings that textual enhancement is effective in helping learners notice the target forms, but is not effective in facilitating the use of target forms. The joint work of rules instruction and textual enhancement has a better effect on both noticing and acquisition of target forms.

Another study conducted by Wong (2002) contrasts the relative effects of sentence-level enhancement and discourse-level enhancement on acquisition of linguistic items. The results indicate that textual enhancement is effective in facilitating language acquisition regardless of whether the input is at the sentence level or the discourse level. The results also show that learners receiving sentence-level input performed better than those who received discourse-level input.

It can be found that the two types of input enhancement, input flood and textual enhancement, are greatly similar in their ways of input provision. The input flood mode aims to increase the exposure frequency of target linguistic items by embedding target items implicitly in the learning materials. The deficiency of this mode is that it is difficult to verify whether learners have noticed the target items and benefited from the input flood. The other input enhancement mode, textual enhancement, successfully compensates this deficiency by using explicit visual manipulating techniques to draw learners' attention to the target items. It seems that the joint work of input flood with explicit textual enhancement will achieve a better effect on drawing learners' attention to the target linguistic items.

3.3.3.3 Data-driven-learning and L2 vocabulary acquisition

As discussed in the previous section, the explicit modification of input by embedding target words into original texts may affect the authenticity of the reading materials. Moreover, it has been verified that the sentence-level input has a better effect on language acquisition than the discourse-level input. Taking the above aspects into consideration, the corpus-based data-driven-learning approach seems to be more appropriate for L2 vocabulary acquisition. A corpus, which is now mainly presented on computers, is a collection of original or natural texts and represents a sample of a particular variety of language. It is originally used by linguists to describe a collection of naturally occurring examples of language and now is widely used in L2 teaching field, especially in vocabulary teaching and learning area. According to Sinclair's (1991) definition, corpus-based data-driven-learning refers to using the computer-generated concordance output to help learners explore the regularities of patterning in the target language and also help teachers develop activities and exercises. This type of data-driven-learning involves the inductive cognitive mode and encourages learners to acquire target linguistic items by inferring and generalizing the meaning or morphosyntactic rules based on their elaborate examination of the authentic materials.

As to L2 vocabulary learning, the data-driven-learning approach has several advantages:

Firstly, learners can be exposed to a battery of authentic example sentences by concordancing the target words in the corpus. In contrast with the input flood approach in which the target words must be artificially embedded into the texts, the data-driven-learning approach can provide authentic sentence-level instances by means of concordance.

Secondly, the target words can be textually enhanced at the sentence level by being presented in the middle of the example sentences with collocated words on the left or right side of the target words. This layout mode of the instance sentence can easily concentrate learners' attention on the target words. It is easier for learners to abstract many aspects of target words' knowledge, such as meaning, collocation, and syntactical features, through instances of encoding in a limited time period.

Thirdly, the collocated words of the target words can be listed in sequence of their appearance frequency. Thus, learners can generalize words that frequently collocate with the target words. Moreover, various example sentences can help learners know the different usages of the target words in different specific contexts.

However, it is also necessary to note that no learning approach is perfect and the data-driven-learning method also has its own drawbacks.

Firstly, although the layout mode of this approach can greatly attract learners' attention to the target words in the example sentences, it seems difficult to control how learners distribute their attention to the different aspects of the target words' knowledge. As discussed in the previous section, depth of word knowledge involves many specific aspects. Learners may pay more attention to one or two aspects of the word knowledge such as its written form or conceptual meaning, but ignore other aspects of the word knowledge. Therefore, explicit instruction is necessary to call learners' attention to certain aspects of word knowledge and help learners develop comprehensive knowledge of the target words.

Secondly, learners may get wrong hypotheses on the meaning or other aspects of target words' knowledge from the instance sentences. It is necessary for the teachers to give feedback on the incorrect generalization or inference by learners.

3.3.4 Output and L2 vocabulary acquisition

3.3.4.1 Theoretical studies on output

3.3.4.1.1 Swain's Output Hypothesis

Before Swain's Output Hypothesis was proposed, Krashen's Input Hypothesis dominated the SLA research field. According to Krashen's Input Hypothesis, the presence of comprehensible input is the only necessary and sufficient condition for SLA. Krashen (1982) holds that learners at stage "i" in their language development can acquire i + 1 by processing i + 1 comprehensible input. Output is regarded as just the natural product of acquisition. With the prevalence of the comprehensible input theory, the immersion education program which aims at providing learners with a target-language exposure learning environment is popular with teachers and parents.

However, the validity of the Input Hypothesis is challenged by Swain (1985) through an evaluation of the immersion program. Swain finds that learners receiving total immersion education performed better on listening and reading comprehension but showed poorer speaking and writing abilities compared with learners not involved in immersion study. A wide range of errors at morpho-syntax level can still be found in the oral or written output by immersion students who have received seven to ten years of extensive daily school instruction. Swain (1985) suggests that despite its importance in the acquisition process, comprehensible input is far from sufficient for learners to fully develop their L2 proficiency. Swain proposes the construct of comprehensible output and assumes that the communicative difficulties will provide students with good opportunities to polish their output to be more precise and appropriate. This language polishing process will greatly facilitate L2 learning.

For the construct of comprehensible output, there are two

misunderstandings which should be clarified. Firstly, comprehensible output refers to the improved version of one's output in terms of its informational content, grammatical, sociolinguistic features rather than the literal meaning—"to be understood" (Van den Branden, 1997). Secondly, many researchers (Pica et al., 1989; Pornpibul, 2002; Shehadeh, 1999, Van den Branden, 1997) consider output as the product rather than the process of language acquisition. However, Swain suggests that the label of "output" in Output Hypothesis should be taken as a practice process which performs several functions to enhance the language development (Swain, 2005).

Swain (1995) identifies four major roles of output in language acquisition: 1) improving learners' fluency; 2) helping learners to notice the gap between what they want to say and what they can say; 3) providing learners with the opportunity to test their hypotheses about their comprehensibility and monitor their linguistic correctness; and 4) helping learners to develop their metalinguistic knowledge of the target language. Firstly, output which is regarded as a practice process can provide opportunities to develop fluent production. Secondly, the noticing function provides learners with opportunities to recognize the problematic areas in their production and to notice the gap between their interlanguage and the target language. In other words, the activity of producing the target language functions is like a trigger to activate the mental processing that may facilitate learners to find and modify their linguistic deficiencies. The cognitive processes prompted by awareness will enhance the generation of newly acquired linguistic knowledge or improve the consolidation of current existing knowledge. Thirdly, the role output plays in language processing is hypothesis testing. Learners acquire linguistic knowledge by first forming hypotheses about the target linguistic items and then testing the validity of their hypotheses according to the feedback from their output. Swain (1995) believes that learners can still test new linguistic forms and structures themselves even if the external feedback is not available for reproduction or modification of their output. In Gass's (1985) SLA model, she also argues that the hypothesis testing facilitates the internalization of the feedback from output into intake. She holds that without the aid of external cues and general world knowledge which can be used in the comprehension process, greater syntactic processing will be involved in production. Fourthly, output activates learners' metalinguistic processing while they are using the target language. Learners can internalize the target language by means of consciously reflecting on their hypotheses about the target language. Reflection on their use of the target language may help learners to be more aware of the grammatical forms, rules and form-function relationships in a communicative context. To explain the reason for unsatisfactory performance on output by learners in an immersion program, Swain argues that output is the necessary condition to push learners to increase control over their learning and possibly overcome the fossilization stage.

In speaking or writing, learners can "stretch" their interlanguage to meet communicative goals. Output may stimulate learners to move from the semantic, open-ended, strategic processing prevalent in comprehension to the complete grammatical processing needed for accurate production. Student' meaningful production of language-output-would thus seem to have a potentially significant role in language development. These characteristics of output provide a justification for its separate consideration, both theoretically and empirically, in an examination of the value of interaction for L2 learning. (Swain, 2000, p. 99)

A great number of empirical studies have verified the distinctive functions of output identified in the Output Hypothesis (e.g., Pica, 1994; Van den Branden, 1997; Izumi & Bigelow 2000; Swain 2000). Although the results of these studies have supported the theoretical arguments in favor of the roles of output in language development, the internal cognitive processes involved in the operation of these output functions have not been discussed in detail. These cognitive processes are discussed in some models based on psycholinguistic and cognitive theories such as Levelt's (1993) Speech Production Model and Anderson's (1983) Skill Learning Model. The following sections will give a general review of these models.

3.3.4.1.2 Levelt's Speech Production Model

Levelt's (1993) Speech Production Model, which was originally constructed to account for L1 adults' speech production, has also been successfully applied to modeling L2 data. In this model, the human brain is viewed as a system which consists of several subcomponents: 1) the conceptualizer, 2) the formulator, 3) the articulator, 4) the acoustic-phonetic processor, and 5) the parser. Besides the five subcomponents, Levelt proposes three distinctive levels representing different sources of knowledge in the production process: 1) the conceptual level, 2) the lemma level, and 3) the word form level. The five subcomponents will function at different levels respectively and jointly to complete a successful speech production.

According to Levelt's model, the message that a speaker intends to convey is primarily generated in the conceptualizer, the product of this stage is called preverbal massage, containing all the information which will be linguistically expressed. Then the preverbal massage is conveyed to formulator to convert the conceptual structure into an articulatory plan. At this level, grammatical encoding is conducted to access the lemmas entailing semantic and syntactic information about lexical items. The syntactic specifications of the selected lemmas will be activated as well. Then the phonological encoding process will be conducted to retrieve a phonetic plan for each lemma. At the third level, the articulator will take the phonetic plan and convert it into the system of actual speech, in which the form and lemma information in the lexicon is retrieved.

Two important features make Levelt's Speech Production Model unique among various processing models. Firstly, his Speech Production Model is highly lexically driven. Lexical selection is a critical factor affecting the functions of other components. Secondly, the speech production involves all subcomponents of processing, which may be recycled to other components. In other words, each component provides necessary information for other components, and the output produced is internally and externally scanned by others.

Although Levelt's model does not account for how language production is acquired, it sheds special light on the functions of output in SLA. Firstly, the description of monitoring in his model supports the claim that language production is not only the result, but also the cause of acquisition. The model gives positive evidence that continuous intervention and recycling between subcomponents are necessary for generating a well-formed and appropriate production. This model also gives support to the assumption that language production is not a one-way liner system but a two-way system involving both output and the concurrent editing or modulation of the output (Scovel, 1998). In other words, the production process, which involves covert or overt self-monitoring of output, enables learners to engage in continuous tuning, feedback, and reorganization. Secondly, in Levelt's model, the speaker who is responsible for message generation and formulation in speech production has less possibility to avoid syntactic operations in the production process. In this sense, the learner is pushed to move from "the semantic processing prevalent in comprehension to the syntactic processing needed for production" (Swain & Lapkin, 1995). Meanwhile, output also forces the learner to activate the morphological and phonological information stored in lexemes, which is accessed only after the semantic information in the lemmas is retrieved (de Bot et al., 1997).

3.3.4.2 Empirical studies on output and L2 vocabulary acquisition

Many studies on the role of output in L2 vocabulary acquisition have been conducted, and the results have been mixed. Some studies have investigated the role of output from the perspective of semantic elaboration and suggest that semantic-oriented output tasks will impede the L2 vocabulary acquisition rates. However, other studies have examined the effects of various types of output activities in the incidental or intentional lexical learning context and shown positive effect on L2 lexical acquisition.

Some researchers explain their studies on the effect of output on L2 lexical acquisition from levels of processing perspective. Prince (1996) compares different L2 lexical rates through translation-based learning and sentence-level contextual learning. He finds that although both of the learning methods associated have semantic elaboration, the translation-based learning method is proved to involve more semantic elaboration process and to be a more effective word learning technique.

Coomber et al. (1986) conducted a study to evaluate the effects of three rehearsal methods (definition, examples, sentence composing, which all involve semantic elaboration) on performance on post-tests after learning. They conclude in their study that increased semantic elaboration does have positive effects on vocabulary learning. They also suggest that compared with definition and examples, sentence composing involves the most semantic processing and is the most effective method. However, Coomber et al.'s findings concluded from this study are interpreted by Barcroft (2004) in an opposite way. Barcroft argues that the definition-based teaching method, which requires meaning comparison actually involves greater semantic elaboration than the sentence composing method. In this case, the better performance of learners receiving the sentence composing method is due to less semantic elaboration involvement. According to Barcroft's analysis, the definition-based teaching method involves greater semantic elaboration than sentence composing, but the degree of semantic elaboration involved in the example method is not mentioned.

If the above two studies exhibit mixed conclusions on the effect of semantic elaboration on L2 word acquisition, the following studies show a definite position that semantic elaboration has no effect or even inhibitory effects on learning new words. In Watanabe's (1997) study, it is suggested that writing the meaning of L2 words in L1 has no obvious effect on lexical acquisition rates. Barcroft (1999) finds that the task of writing new words during word-picture repetition learning will impede word form learning rates. Another study conducted by Barcroft (2004) investigates the effects of sentence writing on L2 lexical acquisition. The results of the study are in line with his previous study and suggest that semantic-oriented sentence writing has inhibitory effects on L2 lexical acquisition. Barcroft (2004) explains these findings with the "type of processing-resource allocation" (TOPRA) model. According to the TOPRA model, semantic elaboration can facilitate learning of the semantic aspects of a target word, but meanwhile can decrease learning of the structural aspects of the word, since the processing-resource is mainly located on semantic processing and little resource can be used in structural processing.

The literature mentioned above suggests the inhibitory role of semantic-oriented output in L2 vocabulary acquisition. However, there are several essential points on these studies' research design part which are ignored in the previous investigation that should be mentioned here to arouse researchers' attention to reinterpret the results of these studies.

Firstly, the semantic-oriented output study actually involves two independent variables, semantic elaboration and output. Many of the studies mentioned above mix the two variables and investigate their joint effect on L2 vocabulary acquisition. For instance, in Barcroft's (2004) study, the sentence-composing task involves not only semantic elaboration, but also structural elaboration such as processing grammatical or morphological features of the target words during the writing process. Both semantic and formal elaborations are involved in the output process, and it's hard to determine which variable plays an inhibitory role in the L2 word acquisition process.

Secondly, some tasks which aim to investigate the role of semantic elaboration in L2 lexical learning rates actually involve no semantic processing. The writing new words task in Barcroft's (1999) study involves mainly formal processing rather than semantic processing. Obviously, performance by learners receiving such a task can only account for the roles of structural elaboration on new word acquisition.

Thirdly, the studies mentioned above have critical defects in their testing instrument, and the findings drawn from these studies cannot be taken as the evidence of the negative effect of semantic-oriented output tasks on L2 vocabulary acquisition. It should be aware that results in these studies are not only determined by the nature of the task types which are semantic-oriented or structural-oriented but also by the test modes adopted in the studies. Studies which compare semantic and non-semantic oriented elaboration treatments all use structural-oriented test instruments and mainly focus on testing learners' formal aspect of word knowledge. Learners who receive semantic-oriented treatment obviously perform not so well in tests which focus on assessing the structural aspect of word knowledge. Barcroft (2004) also admits that the structural test mode can partially account for the negative effect of semantic-oriented output tasks on L2 vocabulary acquisition. Therefore, a multidimensional word knowledge test mode is necessary to test both the formal and semantic aspects of a target word.

Different from studies which focus on the contrast between semantic elaboration and structural elaboration, studies presented in the latter part of this section are conducted from a more general perspective and mainly compare the different effects of input and output tasks on acquisition of L2 receptive and productive word knowledge.

Ellis and He (1999) conducted a comparison study to find the different effects of input and output on the acquisition of receptive and productive vocabularies in L2. Three treatments are compared in their study: 1) premodified input treatment in which the input has been simplified before being exposed to learners; 2) interactionally modified input treatment in which learner can ask the teacher for clarification when they encounter unfamiliar target words before performing the task; and 3) modified output treatment in which learners have to negotiate the meaning of the target words by themselves to complete the task. The results suggest that learners in a modified output treatment outperform learners in the two input groups in the post-test. Therefore, oral interaction can be taken as a beneficial factor which can improve the acquisition of both receptive and productive vocabularies. However, he also indicates that the condition which can clearly distinguish between modified input and modified output is difficult to contrive. Both of the two treatment types involve interaction which consists of input and output processing. In this case, Ellis believes that the positive effects of modified output cannot occur without previous input. The joint work of target word production and negotiation of word meaning are proved to be the most effective in promoting vocabulary acquisition among the three learning conditions.

The following two studies investigate the correlation between production practice and the speed of lexical retrieval. A study conducted by Snellings et al. (2004) shows a positive correlation between the writing task and productive lexical knowledge. In this study, learners given a writing task show a significant improvement in their lexical retrieval speed. Snellings et al. attribute the improved lexical retrieval to narrative writing, because it provides learners in the experimental group with more opportunities to use the target words in their narrative texts.

Another study conducted by Verhallen and Schoonen (1998) also exhibits a positive correlation between output and lexical retrieval. However, learners in their study received the sentence composing task instead of narrative writing. Their findings are in line with Snellings et al.'s (2004) study and support the view that production practice plays an influential role in improving learners' productive aspect of L2 word knowledge.

Acknowledging the positive effects of output on L2 productive word acquisition, some researchers have tried to compare the different effects of various output activities on L2 vocabulary acquisition. Zhang and Wu (2002) have conducted a study to investigate the effects of various instructional techniques on enhancing the productive aspect of word knowledge. Findings in their study suggest that systematic vocabulary instruction which includes reading, writing, and comprehension of the target vocabulary will significantly facilitate receptive vocabulary converting into productive vocabulary. They suggest that writing on a topic related to the reading material provides learners with opportunities to use the target words contextually. Findings in their study support Swain's (1986, 1995) position that the pushed output from learners will enhance L2 lexical acquisition.

A study on the roles of output in L2 vocabulary acquisition conducted by Kwon (2006) involves more variables such as different task sequences and different task modes. Results in her study indicate that learners receiving input and output training performed better in the post word test than learners receiving only input training, but no significant difference had been shown between the input-output task sequence group and the output-input task sequence group. In the peer-interaction group, learners were required to post their written assignment including short answer questions and narrative writings on a web-based bulletin. Learners could see other group members' answers on the bulletin. Through comparing the answers posted by themselves and their peers, learners could refine and repost their answers when they found the errors in their production. Kwon regards this process as online peer-interaction output task mode. Results generated from this experiment indicate that learners in peer-interaction condition performed better the in post test than learners in non-interaction condition, but showed no difference in the writing task which focused on productive vocabulary testing. However, the result can only partially support the hypothesis that peer-interaction output group outperform the non-interaction group. It may be due to the design of the task procedure. Since the learners in the peer-interaction group did not interact with each other synchronously, it is difficult to ensure that every learner read others' productions and made the comparison when they posted their own answers. Besides, as the production was posted after class, it was possible for learners to finish their assignment by consulting the dictionary or other references, the effect of interaction on the acquisition of target words could be intervened by the act of dictionary consulting. Therefore, the efficiency and validity of the so-called peer-interaction need to be further investigated.

However, most studies on the effects of output activities on L2 lexical acquisition are conducted by researchers abroad, and few studies are done in this field in China. Most studies concerning output processing focus on the theoretical analysis and emphasize the importance of output activities in facilitating L2 learning (Feng & Huang, 2004; Zhao, 2004; Zheng, 2005). Few studies in this field include empirical investigation (Cheng, 2003; Zeng, 2005) and empirical studies on the roles of output processing in L2 lexical acquisition are even fewer (Liu, 2006; Song, 2008).

3.4 Conceptual framework for L2 vocabulary acquisition based on Skehan's Information Processing Model

As discussed in previous sections, many cognitive models have given an account of specific stages of the SLA process from distinctive perspectives. Although these cognitive models shed some light on the psychological interpretations for different SLA stages, they fail to present a comprehensive view on the entire learning process. With a comprehensive and thorough survey of the existing cognitive models, Skehan (1998) proposes an information-processing model which entails separate input, central processing and output stages as an integrated sequential process.

According to Skehan, language use and acquisition are constrained by the operation of the information-processing system, which has a limited capacity. He generalizes five features of this system: 1) this system lacks the resources to process all the L2 input received exhaustively (VanPatten, 1990; Doughty, 1991); 2) the system is predisposed to be meaning-oriented at the input stage; 3) information is represented or learned in the form of rule or exemplars in this system; 4) awareness plays an active role in the language system; and 5) lexicalized, exemplar-based representations can be effective for language production under beneficial processing conditions.

In line with Skehan's proposal, the researcher of the present study holds that L2 vocabulary acquisition also follows an integrated information processing flow which involves the apperception of new words, elaboration and integration of target word knowledge into the language system, and using the acquired words in context.

The five features of the information-processing system generalized by Skehan can also provide some inspiration to the L2 vocabulary learning and teaching processes. Firstly, explicit instruction is necessary for information processing since capacity is limited and not all aspects of the input can be completely processed. Secondly, compared with incidental learning which advocates learning words implicitly through reading, the intentional learning and instruction on forms of language is quite critical to compensate the deficient attention to this aspect since the language system prioritizes meaning processing. Thirdly, explicit input enhancement can be conducted to draw learners' attention to the target words or some specific dimensions of the target word knowledge which is easy to be ignored. Fourthly, the exemplar-based inductive learning might be more effective on word knowledge processing than the rule-based deductive learning since vocabulary learning involves more syntactical aspects of word knowledge such as collocation or idioms which do not always follow explicit rules. Fifthly, output plays a critical role in vocabulary acquisition, because it can draw learners' awareness to the target word knowledge they lack, and facilitate the integration of newly acquired word knowledge into their developing mental lexicon.

The present study will explore the roles input and output play in L2 vocabulary acquisition. Different learning conditions based on distinctive cognitive modes for input processing will be compared to find a better way for input processing in L2 vocabulary acquisition. The co-effect of input and output on word learning will also be investigated. Input processing and output will be studied respectively in the two experiments to avoid output becoming an interfering variable in the study of relative effects of different input processing modes on L2 vocabulary acquisition.

Chapter 4 An empirical study on input processing in L2 vocabulary acquisition

4.1 Introduction

This experiment was conducted to compare different effects of various input processing modes on L2 vocabulary acquisition. Three task modes involving three types of input processing ways (inductive processing plus instruction, deductive processing only, inductive processing only) were evaluated to find out which task mode could enhance the L2 vocabulary acquisition best. A brief description of the research design, research questions and hypotheses of the experiment will be given at the beginning of this chapter, followed by the instruction of the procedures of the experiment in detail, such as the participants, experimental materials, target words, test instruments, different task modes and task procedures. Then, experimental results will be reported and discussed based on the data obtained from the experiment.

4.2 Method

4.2.1 Research design and hypotheses

As reviewed in Chapter 2, input plays a critical role in SLA and L2 vocabulary acquisition. Sufficient input can increase the encounter frequency of the target words or other linguistic items for learners. Different types of input can also facilitate learners to learn the different aspects of knowledge or use of a target word in various specific contexts. Hence, many researchers believe that vocabulary should be mainly acquired in the incidental learning context. These researchers claim that the vocabulary acquisition is only a by-product of extensive reading and can be acquired by learners through reading sufficient materials which provide learners with diversified aspects of knowledge of a target word. However, it has been found from many empirical studies that incidental vocabulary learning through purely extensive reading is not an effective way for L2 vocabulary acquisition. There are several reasons for the ineffectiveness of incidental learning. Firstly, it seems too time-consuming for an L2 learner to acquire comprehensive knowledge of a word by reading such a great amount of discourse-level reading materials. Secondly, the learning interval for encountering a target word in different contexts may be so long that learners may have forgotten the word before they have the chance to encounter the word again. Thirdly, it is difficult to ensure that a target word can be noticed and processed thoroughly by learners through extensive reading. Since the main purpose of extensive reading is to comprehend the main idea of the material, not to learn a word, the target word is easily ignored if it won't affect understanding the general meaning of the text. Even if the learners have noticed the word, they mainly assign their attention to the semantic aspect and pay little attention to the word's other knowledge which has no effect on their understanding of the text. Moreover, it is suggested that the discourse-level input is not as effective as the sentence-level input for vocabulary learning since the sentence-level input is shorter and can provide learners with diversified contexts sufficiently in a short time. Therefore, the sentence-level input is suggested to be used as supplementary materials to enhance the efficiency of input exposure.

Besides the different input presenting ways, different cognitive modes may also affect L2 vocabulary acquisition. Two cognitive modes, deductive mode and inductive mode, are involved in the input encoding process. The deductive type of learning mode is widely used in traditional language teaching and learning context in which learners are first presented with the grammatical rules or linguistic items and then asked to encode and memorize the rules or words in the example sentences or reading materials. This type of learning has been criticized for its teacher-centered mode, which is apt to make learners passive knowledge receivers and containers.

In contrast with deductive learning, the inductive learning method is learner-centered. Learners are not firstly exposed to authentic materials rather than the grammatical rules of word knowledge. Learners are asked to generalize the knowledge of the target words or linguistic items from the materials by themselves. The task of the instructor in inductive learning is to attract learners' attention to the multiple aspects of the target word knowledge which are apt to be neglected, and encourage them to use various means to encode and generalize the knowledge of these aspects of the target words. Moreover, it is also necessary for the instructor to provide feedback if learners give inappropriate guessing. Many studies have proved the effectiveness of the inductive mode of learning, especially in the L1 language learning field. However, it seems difficult to ensure that learners notice all the target words and make inductive generalizations of word knowledge from the context.

Based on the theoretical and empirical research on input processing in L2 vocabulary acquisition, research questions and hypotheses are formulated to guide this study. They are formulated based on the assumption that L2 learners' acquisition of target words will be greater by receiving extra deductive information processing or inductive information processing treatment than that under incidental learning context receiving no extra information processing treatment.

1) How do different input processing modes influence L2 vocabulary acquisition of the target words?

2) If there are differences, which mode will enhance L2 vocabulary acquisition of the target words best?

Hypothesis 1: All the three different learning conditions will enhance the target word acquisition.

Hypothesis 2: The intentional learning method will have a better effect on L2 vocabulary acquisition than the incidental learning method.

Hypothesis 2a: Learners receiving the intentional learning treatment will acquire more words than those in the incidental learning context.

Hypothesis 2b: Learners receiving the intentional learning treatment will perform better in the depth of word knowledge test than those in the incidental learning context.

Hypothesis 3: Learners receiving the inductive treatment will perform better on L2 vocabulary acquisition and retention than learners receiving the deductive information processing treatment.

Hypothesis 3a: Learners receiving the inductive treatment will acquire more words than those receiving the deductive information processing treatment.

Hypothesis 3b: Learners receiving the inductive treatment will acquire greater depth of word knowledge than those receiving the deductive information processing treatment.

4.2.2 Subjects

All the 115 participants were freshmen non-English majors enrolled at Zhejiang Sci–Tech University. The participants were all Law majors and came from three parallel classes. At the time of the experiment, they just had two weeks' English lessons at the university. At the beginning of the study, a total of 119 students took part in the pre-test to measure their average vocabulary level; however, during the treatment conducting and post-test process, 4 students in the three classes were absent from the treatment procedures or delayed post-test. Hence, only 115 participants' data were available for the current study. They were randomly divided into four groups, 28 in the inductive group, 29 in the deductive group, 29 in the incidental group, and 29 in the control group.

An English proficiency test was administered to check whether learners in the four groups were at a similar level. The test included four parts, i. e. a multiple choice test for grammatical and word knowledge, a cloze test, a reading comprehension test and writing. The data shown in Table 4-1 below indicates that the mean scores of four groups in this English proficiency test were at a similar level. A further one-way ANOVA (Analysis of Variation) shown in Table 4-2 suggests that there shows no significant differences in the test among the four groups. It proves that the English proficiency of participants in the four groups was at a similar level.

Table 4-1 Descriptive statistics on the English proficiency test for the four groups

Group	*N*	Minimum	Maximum	Mean	Std. deviation
1	28	71.00	98.00	86.2935	9.3610
2	29	65.00	97.00	85.5286	9.5961
3	29	68.00	96.00	85.8795	9.2394
4	29	69.00	95.00	85.9634	8.7539

Note: 1= inductive group, 2= deductive group, 3= incidental group, 4=control group

Table 4-2 One-way ANOVA of the mean scores of the English proficiency test

Group	Sum of squares	*df*	Mean square	*F*	Sig.
Between Groups	7.230	3	0.800	0.500	0.683
Within Groups	535.414	111	4.824		
Total	542.643	114			

The VLT (Nation, 1990) (see Appendix G) was also administered to check whether there were significant differences among the four groups in terms of their vocabulary knowledge. The participants' scores on each level of the VLT and the VLT as a whole were analyzed by using one-way ANOVA. The results shown in Table 4-3 indicate that participants in the four groups showed no significant differences both in the overall vocabulary size and at each word frequency level.

Table 4-3 Comparison of the mean scores in the VLT for the four groups

	1		2		3		4		ANOVA	
Subtest	*M*	*SD*	*M*	*SD*	*M*	*SD*	*M*	*SD*	*M*	*SD*
2000	15.71	1.56	15.26	14.96	14.96	1.12	14.96	2.32	14.96	2.32
3000	12.79	3.66	12.90	12.47	12.47	2.45	12.47	3.41	12.47	3.41
5000	6.42	2.53	6.65	6.03	6.03	3.56	6.03	2.11	6.03	2.11
University	6.00	2.57	5.52	5.39	5.39	4.36	5.39	3.52	5.39	3.52
10,000	4.12	1.45	4.00	3.67	3.67	2.17	3.67	1.91	3.67	1.91
Overall	45.68	8.63	46.24	44.97	44.97	9.25	44.97	6.96	44.97	6.96

Note: 1=inductive group, 2=deductive group, 3=incidental group, 4=control group; 2000=the 2000-word level, 3000=the 3000-word level, 5000=the 5000-word level, university=the university word list level, 10000=the 10000-word level, see Paul Nation's Vocabulary Levels Test (Nation, 1990)

4.2.3 Task modes

Learners in the four groups were assigned different task modes, which differed in their ways of input presentation and cognition modes involved. According to Wong (2005), different ways of textual exposure and enhancement will have different effects on the acquisition of target linguistic items. Learners receiving sentence-level input will perform better in language learning than those with discourse-level input. The various ways of input exposure which involve specific ways of cognitive modes will also affect the effectiveness of L2 vocabulary acquisition. Explicit instruction of the target words before the reading task will lead to the deductive type of intentional learning of target words; while presenting sentence- or discourse-level materials without explicit instruction will lead to the inductive type of implicit learning of the target words. It is also hypothesized that the comprehensive approach involving both inductive and deductive learning will achieve the best effect on L2 vocabulary acquisition. Hence, the co-effects of input presenting mode and cognition mode on L2 word acquisition will be investigated in this study.

Participants in Group 1 were given the comprehensive treatment, involving both inductive learning and explicit instruction. Learners in this group searched for the instances of target words by using the online Corpus of Contemporary American English (COCA) (see Appendix C) which can provide numerous authentic instances excerpted from newspapers, magazines and academic papers. Learners were asked to extract the related word knowledge (such as meaning, synonyms, collocation, grammatical features) and record it on the Word Note (Appendix D). The instructor, also the author of this book, encouraged learners to infer the word meaning by referring to contextual cues or other linguistic hints. Negotiations between learners and the instructor and between learners and their peers were encouraged to achieve the word meaning and other aspects of word knowledge. The wrong inferences would be corrected by the instructor. After learners achieved the correct meaning of the words, the instructor also asked learners to brainstorm other words belonging to the same semantic fields with the new words such as their synonyms or opposites. The semantic features of the words were analyzed not only to help learners achieve a better understanding of the concepts of the new words, but also to find reasons why some words could not collocate with the target words.

In general, although this was an intentional learning process in which learners' attention was drawn to the target words and they were forewarned to be tested on these words, it differed from the typical rule-based intentional learning context in which teachers dominate the learning process. It was a learner-centered approach which encouraged learners to generalize the word knowledge from the input by themselves. Almost all the dimensions of the target word knowledge were required to be generalized by the learners themselves under the supervision of the instructor. The major role the instructor played in this experimental group was to draw learners' attention to some aspects of the words, which were easily to be ignored in incidental learning context, to elicit generalization of the multiple dimensions of the target word knowledge. Meanwhile, the instructor was also responsible for providing corrective feedback when learners gave wrong guessing.

Learners receiving the deductive information processing treatment in Group 2 were given the same reading text attached with a word list (see Appendix E) on which target words' meaning, grammatical categories, collocations and example sentences were provided. Learners were forewarned that words on the list would be tested after the reading task. The instructor gave explicit explanations of target word knowledge to learners.

Learners in Group 3, the incidental learning group, were given the text and reading comprehension task which was the same as Group 1 and Group 2. Two supplementary texts and the corresponding reading comprehension tasks were assigned to them. The target words were not highlighted in the text in this group, and no forewarning about the post vocabulary test was given to learners. In this way, the entire treatment process for learners in Group 3 was very close to the natural incidental learning.

Group 4, the control group, was only provided with the main reading text without a word list or supplementary reading texts.

4.2.4 Experimental materials and target words selection

Reading Passage One (see Appendix A) given to the four groups is a popular science article entitled "London Smog" excerpted from a reading passage in Reading Part of the Test Source for IELTS (Wu, 2005). It gives a vivid description of an abnormal phenomenon caused by the co-effect of air pollution and the special geographical features in London. There are several reasons for choosing this text as the experimental material in this study. Firstly, the genre and difficulty level of the text are similar to the texts in participants' textbook. Secondly, there are several related news reports on this topic written by native speakers, so it's relatively easier to find other two supplementary reading passages for the incidental group, which also contain the target words appearing in the main reading text.

The factor of the coverage rate of the texts had been taken into consideration to ensure the learning context of Group 3 was close to a natural incidental learning setting. According to Laufer (1992) and Nation (1990), the successful guessing of unknown words from the text can occur only when the known word coverage reaches at least 95% to 98%. Some researchers even suggest that the optimal coverage rate of known words in the text should be 96%–99%. Hence, the unknown words in the text should be no more than 5% of the running words in the text, or the successful unfamiliar word meaning inferring will be impossible for the participants.

To verify the coverage rate of known words in the present experimental material, the online software program "Vocabprofile" (Cobb, 2001) was used to check out the frequency of the words in the text. Vocabprofile, based on Laufer and Nation's (1995) Lexical Frequency Profiler, divided the words of texts into four categories by frequency: 1) the most frequent 1000 words of English (i.e., 0–1000), 2) the second most frequent thousand words of English (i.e., 1001–2000), 3) the academic words list of English (short for AWL, 600 words that are frequent in academic texts across subjects), and 4) the remainder which are not found on the other lists.

Posting the original text into the submit window in Vocabprofile, the result showed that 83.32% of the words were from the 0–2000 word frequency range, 4.97% from the academic list, and 12.71% off-list words. From these academic and off-list words, 12 words were selected to be the target words in this experiment, including five verbs, four adjectives, and three nouns. The reason for choosing words belonging to these grammatical categories is that they are active words which are easy to collocate with other words. The number of words in each grammatical category is almost the same, to avoid the unbalance of distribution which might be a variable interfering with the effect of experimental treatment on word acquisition. A close examination of the remaining words in the off-list words pool reveals that most of these are medical terms or unfamiliar place names. The Chinese equivalents of these words were given in the text for each group to make sure the coverage rate of the known words was up to nearly 96%.

Besides Reading Passage One given to all the four groups, two supplementary reading passages (see Appendix B) on the similar topic were also selected as the supplementary materials for Group 3, i.e., the incidental group. These two reading passages also talked about the famous London smog in 1952, excerpted respectively from two popular science articles written by native speakers. The lengths of these two supplementary articles were close to the main experiment text, and all the 12 target words appeared in these texts. The word frequency coverage rates in these articles were also analyzed by Vocabprofile. Except for the 12 target words, other words in the off-list were given with Chinese equivalents to ensure that the known words coverage rates were 97% and 95% respectively.

4.2.5 Task procedures

The treatments for three experimental groups lasted for 45 minutes and the treatment for the control group lasted for only 20 minutes. The study was conducted in four stages as follows:

1. Pre-test: The pre-test consisted of two tests, the vocabulary size test and the test for 12 target words. The vocabulary size test was administered to verify whether participants in the four groups were at the same vocabulary size level. 12 target words mixed with other 14 non-target words were also

tested to find whether participants had acquired these words. The non-target words were used to distract participants' attention to the 12 target words and eliminate the memory effect on the latter study.

2. Treatment conducting: The treatments for the four groups were conducted one week later in their normal class time. First, Groups 1, 3 and 4 were given 10 minutes to read Reading Passage One. Then in the following 35 minutes, participants in Group 1 generalized the multiple aspects of target word knowledge by guessing, analyzing and negotiating with the teacher and their peers, and wrote down all the information about the words on the word note paper. Participants in Group 3 did the reading comprehension task after reading Reading Passage One and reading other supplementary passages, and did the subsequent reading comprehension tasks. Different from the other three groups, participants in Group 2 were given explicit instruction of target word knowledge presented in the word list for 30 minutes. After the word learning, they were asked to read Reading Passage One and do the reading comprehension task.

3. Immediate post-test: Once the tasks were completed, all the experimental materials and note papers were collected and an immediate post-test on the 12 target words was administered to participants of the four groups. The VKS test was used to measure the depth of target word knowledge participants had acquired.

4. Delayed post-test: Nine days after the treatment, the 12 target words were tested again by using the VKS test to gain deeper insights into the effects of different treatments on the retention of the newly acquired words.

4.2.6 Testing instruments and scoring

Three instruments were involved in this experiment. The VLT was used to measure participants' general vocabulary size. The VLT developed by Nation (1990) consists of five subtests, representing five levels of word frequency in

English: the first 2000 words level, the 3000 words level, the 5000 words level, the university word level (beyond 5000 words), and the 10,000 words level. The subtest for each level is composed of six test items. A matching type of items is used, with six words and three meanings in each item.

All the five levels of the VLT were used in this study and one point was awarded to each word, so the maximum total score was 90. Both the mean scores of each group on the VLT and the scores on each level of the VLT were calculated, and an ANOVA was used to verify if there existed a significant difference between the four groups on the vocabulary size.

The VKS (see Appendix H) developed by Paribakht & Wesche (1996) was employed in both the pre-test and two post-tests to measure participants' depth of knowledge of the target words. The test format and way of scoring have been thoroughly discussed in Chapter 2.

Unlike other objective instruments such as multiple choices which have fixed answers, the responses in the VKS are open and may lead to subjectivity in the course of scoring. Therefore, another marker, who is a doctoral candidate and has been teaching English courses for eight years, was invited to mark these tests with the author. According to the pilot marking result, the inter-rater reliability was 0.92. All the responses were marked by two markers independently, and the different scores on the same response would be discussed and remarked again.

The maximum possible score of the 12 target words tested by the VKS was 60 and the minimum possible score was 12 in both pre-test and two post-tests.

Two supplementary tests (see Appendix I) were designed to give detailed information on the acquisition of two subcategories of target word knowledge, the written formal aspect and syntactical (collocation) aspect. The word dictation test was adopted to further testify to the effects of different learning contexts on the acquisition of target words' written form. During the administration of the dictation test, the instructor pronounced each target word in English 3 times and the test-takers were required to write down the correct written form for each word without consultation with the dictionary or text. Correct spelling for each target word would be marked as 1 score, and any wrong spelling in the word would be marked as 0. The maximum possible score of the 12 target words in this dictation test was 12 and the minimum score was 0.

A matching test was designed to compare the effects of different learning contexts on acquisition of collocation knowledge of the target words. In this test, learners were asked to choose the words or phrases which can be collocated with the target words from the 16 alternatives. In these 16 alternatives, 12 of them were correct answers responding to 12 target words respectively, and the other 4 were designed to be distractors to avoid learners obtaining the correct answers by guessing or using other possible strategies. Among the 16 alternatives, some of the alternatives can be used repeatedly to collocate with different target words, but for each target word, one possible collocation with the correct word order provided by the learners was enough. The correct collocates with correct word order would be taken as the correct answer and gain 1 score for each target word; while inappropriate collocation or incorrect word order would be regarded as wrong and gain 0.

The maximum possible score of 12 target words tested by this collocation matching test would be 12 and the minimum possible score would be 0. The reliability for this matching test was 0.83 and the validity 0.85, which indicated this test was reliable and valid in testing the syntactical aspect of word knowledge.

4.2.7 Pilot study

A pilot study was conducted before the formal experiment in three groups. In the pilot study, 32 non-English majors in another class at the same university were grouped into three groups to take part in the pilot experiment. The pilot study was done to fix the time needed for each phase in the experiment and to find whether there would be deficiencies in the task materials or task modes. In this pilot study, 16 words were used as target words, 4 of which seemed to be quite familiar to more than half of the participants. The mean score in the VKS test for each of the 4 words in the pre-test in the pilot study was 3 to 5, which implied that most of the participants had known these words quite well before the experiments. If these 4 words were used in the formal study, it would be difficult to explain whether the possible high mean score of the post-test was determined by the effect of learning context or by learners' previous knowledge about the target words.

Another purpose of the pilot study was to testify whether the test instruments designed for the study were reliable and valid. The VLT and VKL tests were proved to have high reliability and validity as shown in other previous studies. To test the effects of various learning contexts on different dimensions of the target word knowledge, a battery of word knowledge tests was designed and used in this pilot study. These tests were designed according to Nation's (1990) categorization of the dimensions of word knowledge and used to test structural, collocational, and association aspects of target word knowledge. The test for association knowledge was a multiple choice mode consisting of 2 correct associates of each target word and 2 distractors in each item. This test mode is the same as Read's (2000) word association test. However, the result shown in the pilot study revealed that most of the participants gained a quite high score on this test and showed almost no distinction between each other. Therefore, only the dictation test for structural aspect measurement and the matching test for collocational aspect measurement of knowledge were adopted in the previous experiment, and the association test was dropped.

4.3 Results

4.3.1 Results of the overall vocabulary gains

To answer the research questions in this experiment, a battery of statistical analysis was conducted to determine: 1) whether there were any significant changes in the performance within each group over time, and 2) whether there were significant differences in performance between groups after various treatments. Two independent variables and one dependent variable were involved in this experiment. One independent variable was the task mode factor which included three types (inductive learning type, deductive learning type, incidental learning type). The other independent factor was the time factor involving three stages in the vocabulary tests (pre-test, immediate post-test, and delayed post-test). The dependent variable was the vocabulary test. To examine the effect of the independent variables, first, the mean scores for the vocabulary tests were compared. Second, one-way ANOVA was done to verify whether there were any significant differences between the groups for each time and between different times for each group. Thus, the results were presented in the order of 1) descriptive statistics, 2) one-way ANOVA for each of the times and post hoc comparisons, and 3) mean score comparisons between times for each group by using a matching *t*-test. The alpha level for this study was set at 0.05.

4.3.1.1 Comparison of scores on pre-test of VKS for the four groups

The data shown in Table 4-4 indicates that there was no obvious difference among the four groups in their knowledge of the 12 target words. The mean scores of the four groups ranged from 14 to 15, suggesting that most of the target words were quite unfamiliar to the participants. Almost all the participants in these four groups failed to give the correct meaning of the target words, even though they reported that they had seen one or two target words before. The one-way ANOVA shown in Table 4-5 confirms that there was no significant difference among the four groups in the pre-test of the target word knowledge.

Table 4-4 Descriptive statistics on the pre-test of VKS for the four groups

Group	*N*	Minimum	Maximum	Mean	*Std. deviation*
1	28	12.00	18.00	15.0333	1.54213
2	29	12.00	18.00	14.6000	1.63158
3	29	12.00	18.00	14.5600	1.84951
4	29	12.00	18.00	14.0690	1.51023

Note: 1= inductive group, 2= deductive group, 3= incidental group, 4=control group

Table 4-5 One-way ANOVA of the pre-test of VKS for the four groups

Group	Sum of squares	*df*	Mean square	*F*	Sig.
Between groups	16.486	3	5.495	2.063	0.109
Within groups	295.635	111	2.663		
Total	312.122	114			

4.3.1.2 Comparison of scores on immediate post-test between groups

4.3.1.2.1 Comparative results of pre-test and immediate post-test of VKS for each group

The data shown in Table 4-6 suggests that the mean scores for the four groups in the immediate post-test have increased from those in the pre-test. Data presented in Table 4-7 have verified that there was a significant difference (inductive type: t= -62.68, p<0.05; deductive type: t= -36.96, p<0.05; incidental type: t= -21.71, p<0.05) between the scores of pre-test and those of immediate post-test for each group. It suggests participants in all the three experimental groups made great improvement in target word learning. The result verifies Hypothesis 1 that all the three learning contexts would enhance vocabulary acquisition.

Table 4-6 Descriptive statistics on the immediate post-test of VKS test for the four groups

Group	*N*	Minimum	Maximum	Mean	*Std. deviation*
1	28	44.00	55.00	48.8667	2.66178
2	29	31.00	48.00	42.5333	3.54024
3	29	25.00	42.00	34.4000	5.00069
4	29	25.00	38.00	29.8276	3.19675

Note: 1= inductive group, 2= deductive group, 3= incidental group, 4=control group

Table 4-7 Paired sample *t* test of the pre-test and the immediate post-test of VKS for each group

Group	Item	Paired differences				*t*	*df*	Sig.
		Std. deviation	Std. error mean	Confidence interval of the difference				
				Lower	Upper			
1	Pre-test / Post-test 1	2.8552	0.5396	−34.9286	−32.7143	-62.68	27	0.000
2	Pre-test / Post-test 1	4.0796	0.7576	−29.5518	−26.4482	-36.96	28	0.000
3	Pre-test / Post-test 1	4.9780	0.9244	−21.9625	−18.1754	-21.71	28	0.000
4	Pre-test / Post-test 1	3.7669	0.6995	−17.1915	−14.3257	-22.528	28	0.000

Note: 1= inductive group, 2= deductive group, 3= incidental group, 4=control group; post-test 1= immediate post-test

4.3.1.2.2 Comparison of scores on immediate post-test of VKS between groups

Table 4-8 shows that the mean scores for the immediate post-test after the treatments vary greatly between groups. The results show that the mean scores for the four groups in the immediate post-test are all higher than those in the pre-test. It implies that participants in all the four groups gained some knowledge of the target words after the treatment. The mean scores for the three experimental groups are higher than the control group. It suggests that participants receiving three different types of treatments performed better than participants in the control group in the target word knowledge test. Figure

4-1 has presented a clearer illustration of the differences between groups. The mean score for Group 1 ranks the highest among the four groups, followed by Group 2 and Group 3. It suggests that participants in Group 1 performed best in the immediate post-test among the three experimental groups. The mean score for Group 3 is the lowest in the three experimental groups, which implies that participants in the incidental group failed to perform as well as participants in the other two experimental groups in the vocabulary knowledge test. The comparison of mean scores shows the different effects of different treatments, but the specific efficiency of each treatment in facilitating word acquisition has not been shown in previous data analysis. Further one-way ANOVA was also conducted to confirm whether the performances of participants in the four groups were significantly different (Table 4-9).

Table 4-8 Comparison of gains in the immediate post-test of VKS for the four groups

Group	Pre-test	Post-test 1	Gain 1
1	15.0333	48.8667	33.8334
2	14.6000	42.5333	27.9333
3	14.5600	34.4000	19.8400
4	14.0690	29.8276	15.7586

Note: 1= inductive group, 2= deductive group, 3= incidental group, 4=control group; post-test 1= immediate post-test, gain 1= difference gap between post-test 1 and pre-test

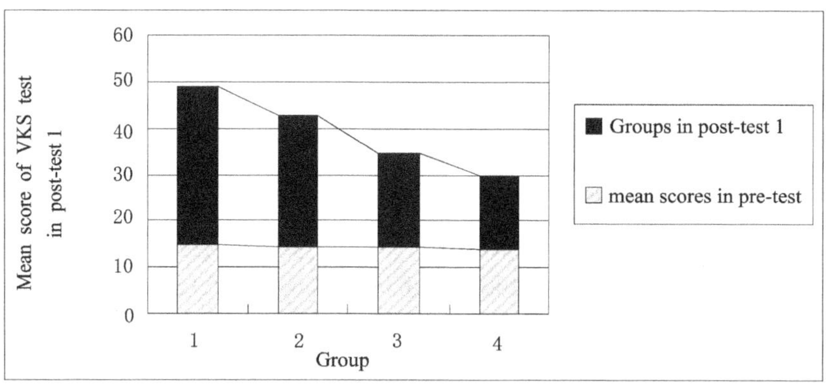

Figure 4-1 Comparison of gains in the immediate post-test of VKS for the four groups

Table 4-9 One-way ANOVA of the immediate post-test of VKS for the four groups

Group	Sum of squares	*df*	Mean square	*F*	Sig.
Between Groups	6123.814	3	2041.271	152.019	0.000
Within Groups	1490.482	111	13.428		
Total	7614.296	114			

Table 4-10 shows that the mean scores for the immediate post-test after the treatments are significantly different between groups. The ANOVA reveals significant differences between each experimental group and the control group. It suggests that participants receiving three different types of treatments all performed better than participants in the control group in the target word knowledge test. It supports Hypothesis 1, which predicts that all the three types of treatments have a positive effect on vocabulary acquisition. Although three experimental treatments all show a positive effect on target vocabulary learning, the effectiveness of these methods varies greatly. The significant differences between Group 1 and Group 3 (p=0.000 < 0.05) and between Group 2 and Group 3 (p=0.000 < 0.05) suggest that participants receiving comprehensive or deductive treatment performed better in word knowledge test than those receiving incidental treatment. Hence, Hypothesis 2, which predicts that both the comprehensive treatment and deductive treatment have a better effect on L2 vocabulary acquisition than the purely inductive incidental learning method is verified. The significant difference between Group 1 and Group 2 (p=0.000 < 0.05) supports Hypothesis 3, which predicts that the comprehensive treatment has a better effect than the deductive treatment on L2 vocabulary acquisition.

Table 4-10 Scheffe post hoc comparison of mean scores of the immediate post-test of VKS for the four groups

Group		Mean difference (I-J)	Std. error	Sig.	95% confidence interval	
					Lower bound	Upper bound
1	2	6.41256*	0.97087	0.000	3.6564	9.1687
	3	14.27463*	0.97087	0.000	11.5185	17.0308
	4	19.13670*	0.97087	0.000	16.3805	21.8929
2	1	−6.41256*	0.97087	0.000	−9.1687	−3.6564
	3	7.86207*	0.96232	0.000	5.1302	10.5940
	4	12.72414*	0.96232	0.000	9.9923	15.4560
3	1	−14.27463*	0.97087	0.000	−17.0308	−11.5185
	2	−7.86207*	0.96232	0.000	−10.5940	−5.1302
	4	4.86207*	0.96232	0.000	2.1302	7.5940
4	1	−19.13670*	0.97087	0.000	−21.8929	−16.3805
	2	−12.72414*	0.96232	0.000	−15.4560	−9.9923
	3	−4.86207*	0.96232	0.000	−7.5940	−2.1302

*. The mean difference is significant at the 0.05 level.

Note: 1= inductive group, 2= deductive group, 3= incidental group, 4=control group

4.3.1.3 Comparison of scores on delayed post-test for the four groups

4.3.1.3.1 Comparative results of the pre-test and the delayed post-test of VKS for each group

The delayed post-test was administrated nine days later to the four groups without forewarning, to investigate the relative effects of treatments on vocabulary retention. Results of the descriptive data of the mean scores for the four groups in the delayed post VKS test shown in Table 4-11 indicate that all the four groups had some retention of the acquired knowledge of the target words to different degrees. A battery of data analysis was conducted to further investigate whether there were significant differences between the pre-test and delayed post-test and among the four groups. Paired Sample *t* Test was first conducted to verify the significance of the differences between the pre-test and delayed post-test for each group.

Table 4-11 Descriptive statistics on the delayed post-test of VKS for the four groups

Group	*N*	Minimum	Maximum	Mean	std. deviation
1	28	40.00	52.00	44.9333	2.92355
2	29	25.00	42.00	35.9000	3.85379
3	29	21.00	37.00	29.3000	4.37981
4	29	24.00	33.00	26.8276	2.49383

Note: 1= inductive group, 2= deductive group, 3= incidental group, 4=control group

The results of paired sample *t* test shown in Table 4-12 indicate that there were significant differences between the pre-test and the delayed post-test for the four groups. It suggests that the three types of treatments all had positive effects on retention of the newly learned word knowledge. Hypothesis 1, which predicts that three types of treatment all have a positive effect on L2 vocabulary acquisition, is supported again.

Table 4-12 Paired sample *t* test of the pre-test and the delayed post-test of VKS for each group

Group	Item	Paired differences				*t*	*df*	Sig. (2-tailed)
		Std. deviation	Std. error mean	95% confidence interval of the difference				
				Lower	Upper			
1	Pre-test / Post test 2	3.20940	0.60652	−30.92305	−28.43410	−48.933	27	0.000
2	Pre-test / Post-test 2	3.68662	0.68459	−22.74714	−19.94251	−31.179	28	0.000
3	Pre-test / Post-test 2	4.31546	0.80136	−16.50358	−13.22586	−18.546	28	0.000
4	Pre-test / Post-test 2	2.94782	0.54740	−13.87991	−11.63733	−23.308	28	0.000

Note: 1= inductive group, 2= deductive group, 3= incidental group, 4=control group, post-test 2= delayed post-test

4.3.1.3.2 Comparison of scores on the delayed post-test for the four groups

Table 4-13 shows the comparison of gains in the post-test for the four groups. It can be found from Figure 4-2 that the mean score for the inductive group is still the highest among the four groups, followed by the deductive group. The incidental group has the least retention of the target word knowledge among the three experimental groups. Figure 4-3 shows the difference gap between the delayed post-test and the immediate post-test of the four groups. The results indicate that the mean score of the deductive group decreases to the greatest extent among the four groups. It suggests that the deductive learning context is not as effective as the inductive group in facilitating the retention of the acquired L2 vocabulary knowledge.

Table 4-13 Comparison of gains in the delayed post-test for the four groups

Group	Pre-test	Post-test 1	Post-test 2	Gain 2	Lost score
1	15.0333	48.8667	44.9333	29.9000	3.9344
2	14.6000	42.5333	35.9000	21.3000	6.6333
3	14.5600	34.4000	29.3000	14.7400	5.1000
4	14.0690	29.8276	26.8276	12.7586	2.9994

Note: 1= inductive group, 2= deductive group, 3= incidental group, 4=control group; gain2 = difference gap between post-test 2 and pre-test; lost score= difference gap between post-test 2 and post-test 1

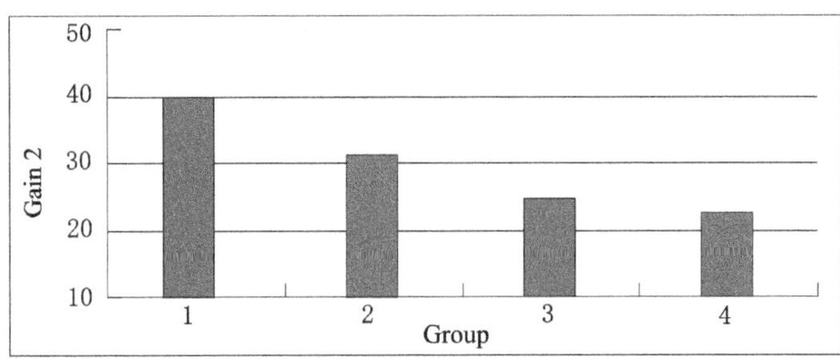

Figure 4-2 Comparison of gains in the delayed post-test for the four groups

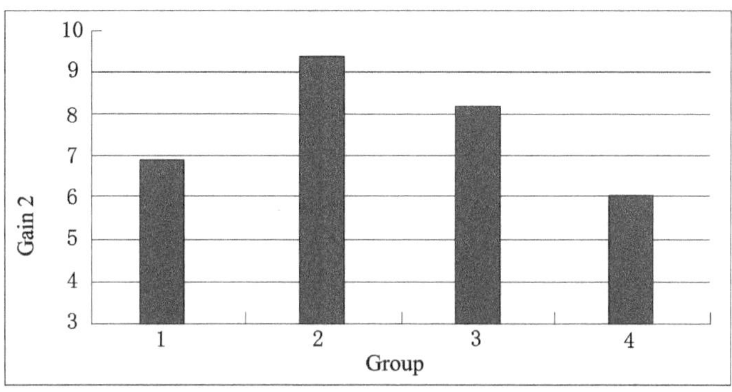

Figure 4-3 Comparison of lost scores in the delayed post-test for the four groups

The one-way ANOVA shown in Table 4-14 reveals that mean scores of Group 1 and Group 2 are significantly higher than that of the incidental group. It suggests that the inductive treatment and the deductive treatment have a better effect on the retention of vocabulary knowledge than the incidental learning method. Moreover, Table 4-15 shows that the inductive group is more effective on word knowledge retention than the deductive group (p=0.000<0.05). However, there shows no significant difference between the incidental group and the control group. It implies that the incidental type treatment has no obvious enhancement on retention of L2 vocabulary knowledge (p=0.057>0.05). Hence, Hypothesis 1 is only partially supported.

Table 4-14 One-way ANOVA of the delayed post-test of VKS for the four groups

Group	Sum of squares	*df*	Mean square	*F*	Sig.
Between groups	5482.518	3	1827.506	145.731	0.000
Within groups	1391.969	111	12.540		
Total	6874.487	114			

Table 4-15 Scheffe post hoc comparison of mean scores of the delayed post-test for the four groups

Group		Mean difference (I-J)	Std. error	Sig.	95% confidence interval	
					Lower bound	Upper bound
1	2	8.92488*	0.93824	0.000	6.2613	11.5884
	3	15.40764*	0.93824	0.000	12.7441	18.0712
	4	17.99384*	0.93824	0.000	15.3303	20.6574
2	1	−8.92488*	0.93824	0.000	−11.5884	−6.2613
	3	6.48276*	0.92997	0.000	3.8427	9.1228
	4	9.06897*	0.92997	0.000	6.4289	11.7090
3	1	−15.40764*	0.93824	0.000	−18.0712	−12.7441
	2	−6.48276*	0.92997	0.000	−9.1228	−3.8427
	4	2.58621	0.92997	0.057	−0.0539	5.2263
4	1	−17.99384*	0.93824	0.000	−20.6574	−15.3303
	2	−9.06897*	0.92997	0.000	−11.7090	−6.4289
	3	−2.58621	0.92997	0.057	−5.2263	0.0539

*. The mean difference is significant at the 0.05 level.

Note: 1= inductive group, 2= deductive group, 3= incidental group, 4=control group

In summary, a general data analysis of the mean scores of three vocabulary knowledge tests for the four groups supports the predication of Hypothesis 2 and Hypothesis 3, but only partially supports Hypothesis 1. The significant differences in the pre-test and the immediate post-test of the three experimental groups have proved that all the three learning contexts can facilitate L2 vocabulary learning. However, the results of the delayed post-test suggest that words memorized by participants in the incidental group decreased and were finally retained as few as the control group. The participants performing extra information processing tasks performed better in the vocabulary knowledge test than participants in purely incidental learning context. The inductive group performed best among the three experimental groups.

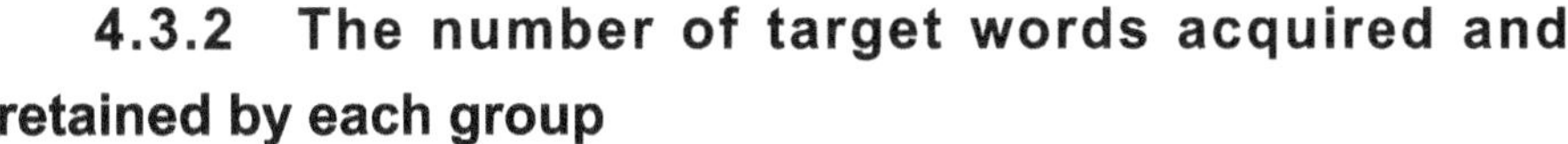

4.3.2 The number of target words acquired and retained by each group

The previous sections have given a comparison of the general gains of the target words by different groups, but the number of target words acquired and retained by participants in each group cannot be inferred from the previous analysis. The scoring method for the VKS test then was adjusted to articulate the concrete number of target vocabulary acquired and retained in each group. Since the scores of 1 and 2 in the VKS test stand for the test takers' failure to provide a correct meaning of the prompt word, it suggests that the test takers have no knowledge of the word; and the scores of 3–5 indicate that the test takers can provide partial or comprehensive knowledge of the prompt word such as the meaning, collocation or grammatical features of that word. Thus, the original five-scale scoring type was transformed into two scales. The scores of 1–2 in previous data were converted into 0, representing failing to acquire any target word knowledge, and the scores of 3–5 were all converted into 1, symbolizing partial or full acquisition of the target word knowledge. The way of adjustment for the scoring system was used in Wang's (2005) study and proved to be reliable and valid to measure the number of target word acquisition. Based on this new scoring system, the maximum score for each test with 12 target words was 12 and the minimum score was 0. The mean scores of acquired word number for each group in each VKS test are shown in Table 4-16.

It can be found from Table 4-16 that participants in three experimental groups gained more words than the control group. Both the inductive group and the deductive group gained more words than the incidental group. However, as shown in Figure 4-4, there seems no obvious difference in the number of acquired words between the inductive group and the deductive group. This finding is inconsistent with the previous findings from the analysis of the VKS test results. Meanwhile, the results of post-test shown in Figure 4-5 indicate that the inductive group retained as many words as the deductive group. The follow-up one-way ANOVA of the number of the acquired words was conducted to further measure whether the numbers of words acquired by different groups were significantly different.

Table 4-16 Descriptive statistics on the number of words for the four groups in three tests

	1		2		3		4	
Vocabulary test	*M*	*SD*	*M*	*SD*	*M*	*SD*	*M*	*SD*
Pre-test	0.21	0.42	0.15	0.39	0.17	0.24	0.11	0.16
Post-test 1	9.07	1.84	8.73	1.55	5.35	1.12	2.17	1.41
Post-test 2	7.43	1.55	7.00	1.75	2.83	1.47	1.76	1.29

Note: 1= inductive group, 2= deductive group, 3= incidental group, 4=control group

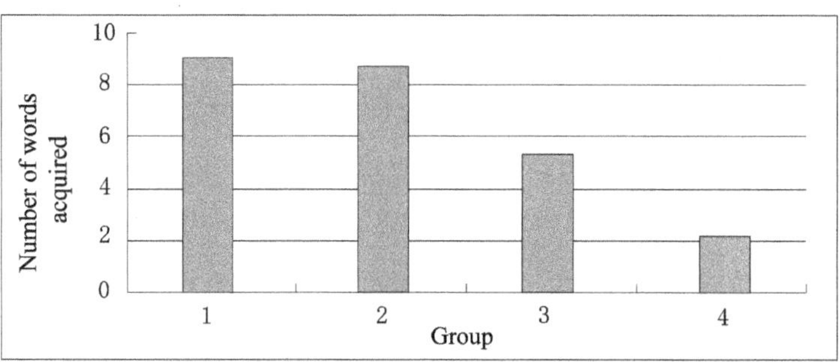

Figure 4-4 Comparison of the number of words acquired by the four groups

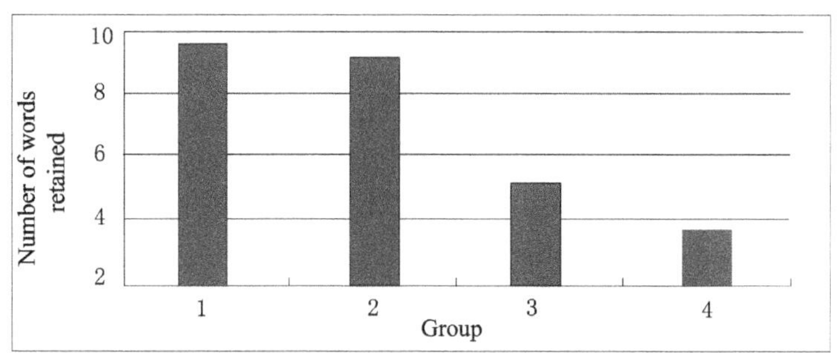

Figure 4-5 Comparison of the number of words retained by the four groups

Data shown in Table 4-17 have verified that all the three experimental groups performed significantly better than the control group in target word acquisition and retention. Moreover, it also proves that the target words acquired by both inductive and deductive groups are more than that of the incidental group. Hypothesis 2 is supported again. However, data for the comparison of the inductive group and the deductive group in Table 4-18 fail to present sound support for Hypothesis 3a, which predicts that the inductive group will acquire and retain more words than the deductive group. Although the number of target words acquired by the inductive group was slightly bigger than that of the deductive group, the difference failed to reach the significant value (p=0.771> 0.05). Moreover, the data in Table 4-20 indicate that there is no significant difference between the two groups in the delayed post-test. Therefore, Hypothesis 3a is not supported by the results. Data in Table 4-20 also indicate that there is no significant difference between the incidental group and the control group.

Table 4-17 One-way ANOVA of the number of words acquired in the immediate post-test

Group	Sum of squares	*df*	Mean square	*F*	Sig.
Between groups	945.694	3	315.231	133.414	0.000
Within groups	262.271	111	2.363		
Total	1207.965	114			

Table 4-18 Scheffe post hoc comparison of the number of words acquired by the four groupsin the immediate post-test

Group		Mean difference (I-J)	Std. error	Sig.	95% confidence interval	
					Lower bound	Upper bound
1	2	0.55419	0.40726	0.605	−0.6020	1.7103
	3	4.65764*	0.40726	0.000	3.5015	5.8138
	4	6.89901*	0.40726	0.000	5.7429	8.0552
2	1	−0.55419	0.40726	0.605	−1.7103	0.6020
	3	4.10345*	0.40367	0.000	2.9575	5.2494
	4	6.34483*	0.40367	0.000	5.1989	7.4908

Continued

Group		Mean difference (I-J)	Std. error	Sig.	95% confidence interval	
					Lower bound	Upper bound
3	1	−4.65764*	0.40726	0.000	−5.8138	−3.5015
	2	−4.10345*	0.40367	0.000	−5.2494	−2.9575
	4	2.24138*	0.40367	0.000	1.0954	3.3874
4	1	−6.89901*	0.40726	0.000	−8.0552	−5.7429
	2	−6.34483*	0.40367	0.000	−7.4908	−5.1989
	3	−2.24138*	0.40367	0.000	−3.3874	−1.0954

*: The mean difference is significant at the 0.05 level.

Note: 1= inductive group, 2= deductive group, 3= incidental group, 4=control group

Table 4-19 One-way ANOVA of the number of words remained in the delayed post-test

Group	Sum of squares	*df*	Mean square	*F*	Sig.
Between Groups	714.338	3	238.113	102.323	0.000
Within Groups	258.305	111	2.327		
Total	972.643	114			

Table 4-20 Scheffe post hoc comparison of the number of words retained in the delayed post-test

Group		Mean difference (I-J)	Std. error	Sig.	95% confidence interval	
					Lower bound	Upper bound
1	2	0.42857	0.40417	0.771	−0.7188	1.5760
	3	4.60099*	0.40417	0.000	3.4536	5.7484
	4	5.66995*	0.40417	0.000	4.5226	6.8173
2	1	−0.42857	0.40417	0.771	−1.5760	0.7188
	3	4.17241*	0.40061	0.000	3.0351	5.3097
	4	5.24138*	0.40061	0.000	4.1041	6.3787
3	1	−4.60099*	0.40417	0.000	−5.7484	−3.4536
	2	−4.17241*	0.40061	0.000	−5.3097	−3.0351
	4	1.06897	0.40061	0.074	−0.0683	2.2062
4	1	−5.66995*	0.40417	0.000	−6.8173	−4.5226
	2	−5.24138*	0.40061	0.000	−6.3787	−4.1041
	3	−1.06897	0.40061	0.074	−2.2062	0.0683

*: The mean difference is significant at the 0.05 level.

Note: 1= inductive group, 2= deductive group, 3= incidental group, 4=control group

4.3.3 Comparison of depth of vocabulary knowledge acquired by three experimental groups

4.3.3.1 Comparison of depth of vocabulary knowledge according to the result of the VKS test

The previous sections have compared the performance of the three groups in the general target word knowledge test and the specific number of target words acquired and retained. The results have revealed that all the three learning contexts have a positive effect on improving target word acquisition. The data have also identified that the inductive and deductive groups performed better than the incidental group in both the general target word knowledge test and the number of target words acquired and retained. Thus, both Hypothesis 1 and Hypothesis 2 are fully confirmed to be true. However, for the inductive and deductive groups, although the inductive group performed significantly better in the VKS test of the target words than the deductive group, the quantity of target words acquired and retained by the two groups shows no significant differences. The inconsistency between results in the two modes of vocabulary measures makes it decide whether Hypothesis 3 is true or not. As Nation (1990) argues, the full acquisition of a word includes not only knowing its meaning or L1 equivalent but also other multiple aspects of the word knowledge such as its conceptual, collocational, syntactical or functional features. Therefore, to draw a conclusion only by assessing the overall gains and the number of words acquired and retained is not convincing. Depth of word knowledge acquired needs to be identified to achieve a more comprehensive understanding of the effects on word acquisition in the two learning contexts.

One of the advantages of the VKS test instrument is that it not only assesses the general acquisition of the target word knowledge, but also tracks the acquisition process and identifies the specific depth of test takers' word knowledge. The five categories respectively stand for different depth of word knowledge. To compare the differences in depth of target word knowledge acquired by the four groups, the scores for each target word in each test were grouped to check the frequency distribution of each category in the three tests for each group. The results are presented in Table 4-21.

Table 4-21 Frequency distribution of the 5 scoring categories in the pre- and post-VKS tests

		VKS scoring categories				
Test	Group	Category 1	Category 2	Category 3	Category 4	Category 5
Pre-test	1	72.3%	27.1%	0.6%		
	2	79.6%	19.7%	0.3%		
	3	81.5%	17.6%	0.7%	0.2%	
	4	75.7%	23.4%	0.8%		0.1%
Immediate	1		23.7%	2.6%	5.6%	68.1%
post-test	2		25.6%	1.9%	29.2%	42.3%
	3	12.7%	38.8%	31.6%	5.2%	11.7%
	4	26.9%	52.2%	4.6%	8.4%	7.9%
Delayed	1	8.2%	30.6%	2.1%	27.9%	39.2%
post-test	2	9.6%	32.1%	17.4%	21.3%	19.6%
	3	15.4%	52.7%	26.2%	4.7%	16.4%
	4	21.6%	47.3%	16.7%	3.2%	11.2%

Note: 1= inductive group, 2= deductive group, 3= incidental group, 4=control group

Firstly, it can be found from Table 4-21 that all the participants' knowledge of almost all the target words in the pre-test fell into Categories 1 and 2, which means participants in the three experimental groups did not know or had not seen these target words at the beginning of the experiment. Secondly, the results for categories distribution in the immediate post-test for each group show the great difference between groups. For the inductive group, more than 70% of scores for the target words fell in Categories 4 and 5, which were much higher than the scores of the deductive group and incidental group; while for the deductive group, most of the target words fell in Category 3. The implication is that the knowledge of the target words acquired by the deductive group was only in the meaning aspect and other dimensions of the target word knowledge had not been acquired. The contrast on category distribution between the inductive and deductive groups reveals that although there is no significant difference in the number of acquired words from the previous superficial investigation, depth of knowledge of target words acquired is different to a great extent between the inductive group and the deductive group. Word knowledge acquired by the deductive group is relatively shallower than that by the deductive group (see Figure 4-6 and Figure 4-7).

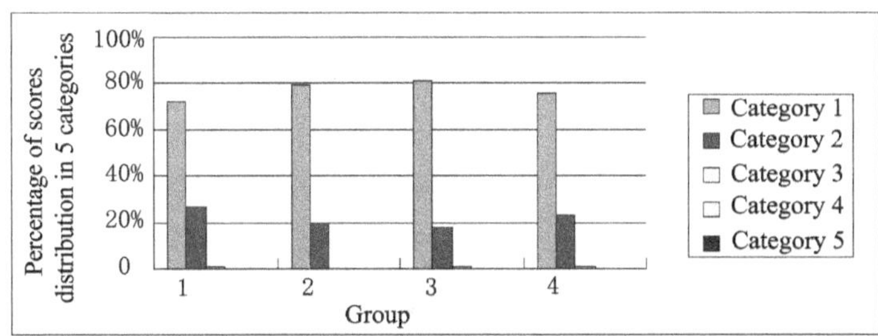

Figure 4-6 Categories distribution in the pre-test for the four groups

Note: 1= inductive group, 2= deductive group, 3= incidental group, 4=control group

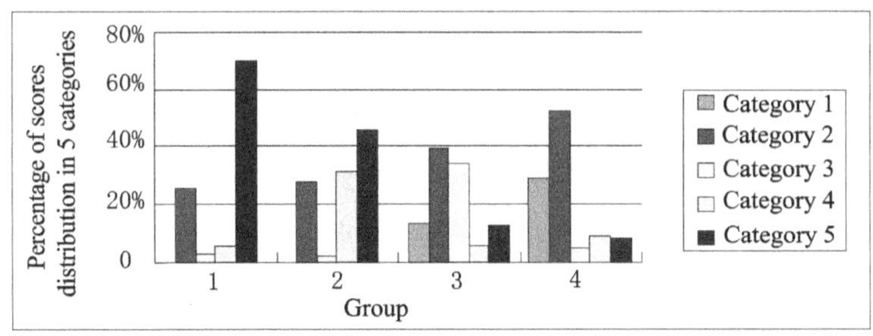

Figure 4-7 Categories distribution in the immediate post-test for the four groups

Note: 1= inductive group, 2= deductive group, 3= incidental group, 4=control group

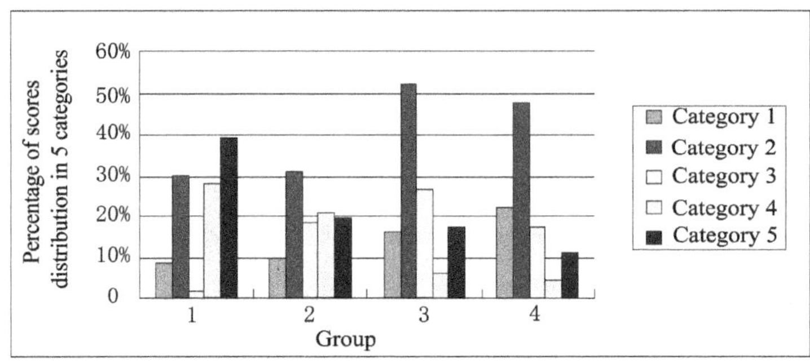

Figure 4-8 Categories distribution in the delayed post-test for the four groups

Note: 1= inductive group, 2= deductive group, 3= incidental group, 4=control group

4.3.3.2 Comparison of the structural aspect of word knowledge acquired by the four groups

To obtain some detailed and supplementary information about the effectiveness of different learning contexts on the acquisition of formal aspect of knowledge, a one-way ANOVA was conducted to find whether it shows significant differences in the scores of the dictation test between groups.

The descriptive data shown in Table 4-22 indicate that mean scores of the learners in both the inductive group and deductive group are close to 9, which means most of them have acquired about 75% of the target words in the form aspect and achieved good acquisition of the written form of the target words. In contrast, for the learners in the incidental group, their mean score is only 3.20, which suggests they only acquired around 25% of the target words in the form aspect. The results of further post hoc multiple comparisons prove that there exists a significant difference between the four groups (p=0.000, post hoc scheffe p<0.05). The data suggest that all the three experimental groups gained better structural knowledge than the control group. Hypothesis 1 is verified here again. Both the inductive group and the deductive group performed better in two dictation post tests than the incidental group (see Table 4-23 and Table 4-24). Hence, Hypothesis 2b is proved to be true. However, the data show that the deductive group performed better in the immediate post dictation test than the inductive group and performed as well as the inductive group in the delayed post test. Hence, Hypothesis 2b, which predicts that the inductive group will gain greater depth of word knowledge, cannot be supported by the findings in the formal aspect of word knowledge.

Table 4-22 Descriptive statistics on the dictation tests for the four groups

	Group 1		Group 2		Group 3		Group 4	
Vocabulary test	*M*	*SD*	*M*	*SD*	*M*	*SD*	*M*	*SD*
The post-test 1	8.46	1.17	9.38	1.42	3.20	1.01	1.66	1.31
The post-test 2	6.64	1.31	6.71	1.33	2.65	1.26	1.37	1.05

Table 4-23 Multiple comparisons of mean scores of the dictation tests for the four groups

Group		Mean difference	Std. error	Sig.	95% confidence interval	
					Lower bound	Upper bound
1	2	-0.91502*	0.31520	0.043	-1.8098	-0.0202
	3	5.25739*	0.31520	0.000	4.3626	6.1522
	4	6.80911*	0.31520	0.000	5.9143	7.7039
2	1	0.91502*	0.31520	0.043	0.0202	1.8098
	3	6.17241*	0.31242	0.000	5.2855	7.0593
	4	7.72414*	0.31242	0.000	6.8372	8.6111
3	1	-5.25739*	0.31520	0.000	-6.1522	-4.3626
	2	-6.17241*	0.31242	0.000	-7.0593	-5.2855
	4	1.55172*	0.31242	0.000	0.6648	2.4387
4	1	-6.80911*	0.31520	0.000	-7.7039	-5.9143
	2	-7.72414*	0.31242	0.000	-8.6111	-6.8372
	3	-1.55172*	0.31242	0.000	-2.4387	-0.6648

*. The mean difference is significant at the 0.05 level.

Note: 1= inductive group, 2= deductive group, 3= incidental group, 4=control group

Table 4-24 Multiple comparisons of mean scores of the delayed post dictation test for the four groups

Group		Mean difference	Std. error	Sig.	95% confidence interval	
					Lower bound	Upper bound
1	2	−0.66749	0.32982	0.257	−1.6038	0.2688
	3	3.98768*	0.32982	0.000	3.0514	4.9240
	4	5.26355*	0.32982	0.000	4.3272	6.1999
2	1	0.66749	0.32982	0.257	−0.2688	1.6038
	3	4.65517*	0.32692	0.000	3.7271	5.5832
	4	5.93103*	0.32692	0.000	5.0030	6.8591
3	1	−3.98768*	0.32982	0.000	−4.9240	-3.0514
	2	−4.65517*	0.32692	0.000	−5.5832	-3.7271
	4	1.27586*	0.32692	0.002	0.3478	2.2039
4	1	−5.26355*	0.32982	0.000	−6.1999	−4.3272
	2	−5.93103*	0.32692	0.000	−6.8591	−5.0030
	3	−1.27586*	0.32692	0.002	−2.2039	-0.3478

*. The mean difference is significant at the 0.05 level.

Note: 1= inductive group, 2= deductive group, 3= incidental group, 4=control group

4.3.4 Comparison of collocational aspect of word knowledge acquired by three experimental groups

A one-way ANOVA was conducted to testify whether learners in the inductive and deductive groups would perform, better in word knowledge acquisition on collocational dimension than those in the incidental group.

Data shown in Table 4-25 suggest that the inductive group performed the best in the collocation test and the mean score of learners in this group is 8.25, followed by the deductive group, whose mean score is 7.86, and the mean score of the incidental group is only 3.07, raking the lowest among three groups. The mean scores of the inductive group and the deductive group are significantly higher than that of the incidental group. It implies that the inductive and deductive learning contexts are better in facilitating depth of word knowledge acquisition in the collocation aspect than the incidental learning context. The followed post hoc multiple comparisons shown in Table 4-26 and Table 4-27 have verified that learners in the three experimental groups performed significantly different in their performance in both the immediate and delayed collocation matching test. However, Table 4-28 exhibits no significant difference in the performance in the immediate post-test between the inductive group and the deductive group. In Table 4-29, the comparison of the mean scores in the delayed post-test shows that there is significant difference between the two groups. It suggests that the inductive treatment is no more effective than the deductive treatment in improving the acquisition of collocation aspect of knowledge, but it is more effective than the deductive treatment in facilitating the retention of this aspect of vocabulary knowledge.

Table 4-25 Descriptive statistics on the collocation match test for the four groups

	Group 1		Group 2		Group 3		Group 4	
Vocabulary test	*M*	*SD*	*M*	*SD*	*M*	*SD*	*M*	*SD*
Post-test 1	8.25	1.86	7.86	1.92	3.07	1.13	1.48	1.27
Post-test 2	6.64	1.31	4.39	1.56	2.42	1.48	1.15	1.21

Table 4-26 One-way ANOVA of the immediate collocation match test for the four groups

Group	Sum of squares	*df*	Mean square	*F*	Sig.
Between groups	997.972	3	332.657	220.051	0.000
Within groups	167.802	111	1.512		
Total	1165.774	114			

Table 4-27 One-way ANOVA of the delayed collocation match test for the four group

Group	Sum of squares	*df*	Mean square	*F*	Sig.
Between groups	505.995	3	168.665	156.214	0.000
Within groups	120.927	112	1.080		
Total	626.922	114			

Table 4-28 Multiple comparisons of mean scores of the immediate collocation match test for the four groups

Group		Mean difference	Std. error	Sig.	95% confidence interval	
					Lower bound	Upper bound
1	2	0.38793	0.32576	0.702	−0.5369	1.3127
	3	5.18103*	0.32576	0.000	4.2562	6.1058
	4	6.76724*	0.32576	0.000	5.8425	7.6920
2	1	−0.38793	0.32576	0.702	−1.3127	0.5369
	3	4.79310*	0.32289	0.000	3.8765	5.7097
	4	6.37931*	0.32289	0.000	5.4627	7.2959
3	1	−5.18103*	0.32576	0.000	−6.1058	−4.2562
	2	−4.79310*	0.32289	0.000	−5.7097	−3.8765
	4	1.58621*	0.32289	0.000	0.6696	2.5028
4	1	−6.76724*	0.32576	0.000	−7.6920	−5.8425
	2	−6.37931*	0.32289	0.000	−7.2959	−5.4627
	3	−1.58621*	0.32289	0.000	−2.5028	−0.6696

*: The mean difference is significant at the 0.05 level.

Note: 1= inductive group, 2= deductive group, 3= incidental group, 4=control group

Table 4-29 Multiple comparisons of mean scores of the delayed collocation match test for the four groups

Group		Mean difference	Std. error	Sig.	95% confidence interval	
					Lower bound	Upper bound
1	2	2.22660*	0.27530	0.000	1.6811	2.7721
	3	4.22660*	0.27530	0.000	3.6811	4.7721
	4	5.53810*	0.27304	0.000	4.9971	6.0791
2	1	−2.22660*	0.27530	0.000	2.7721	−1.6811
	3	2.00000*	0.27288	0.000	1.4593	2.5407
	4	3.31149*	0.27059	0.000	2.7753	3.8476
3	1	−4.22660*	0.27530	0.000	−4.7721	−3.6811
	2	−2.00000*	0.27288	0.000	−2.5407	−1.4593
	4	1.31149*	0.27059	0.000	0.7753	1.8476
4	1	−5.53810*	0.27304	0.000	−6.0791	−4.9971
	2	−3.31149*	0.27059	0.000	−3.8476	−2.7753
	3	−1.31149*	0.27059	0.000	−1.8476	−0.7753

*: The mean difference is significant at the 0.05 level.

Note: 1= inductive group, 2= deductive group, 3= incidental group, 4=control group

4.4 Discussion

4.4.1 Discussion of Hypothesis 1

Hypothesis 1 predicts that the three different learning conditions will all enhance the target word acquisition. The prediction is verified through a battery of data analyses. The number of target words acquired by each group before the treatments is close to 0. However, as Table 4-9 and Table 4-10 have shown, all the three groups acquired some target word knowledge to different extent in the immediate post-tests after the treatments.

This result confirms Craik's (1976) claims about levels of processing. Craik differentiates two levels of information processing: Structural level and semantic level. The information processing on the semantic level has been proved to leave deeper traces in human's memory system than the information processing on the structural level in his study. Thus, Craik argues that structural encoding is only the superficial level of information processing and has little effect on long-term memory retention; while semantic encoding is a much deeper level of information processing and is more beneficial for long-term memory retention. According to Craik's proposition, the word learning tasks which involve semantic encoding have a better effect on word retention than tasks involving structural encoding.

All the three learning contexts in this study were associated with semantic encoding of the target words. The inductive information processing task designed for Group 1 required participants to guess the meaning of the target words by referring to the main text and the instances first, and feedback was provided to help participants evaluate the meaning of the target words by comparing their guessing with the feedback. Semantic encoding was conducted through both the guessing and evaluation processes. For participants in Group 2, the deductive information processing task in which the meaning of target words had been provided also required them to encode the semantic aspect of the target words in reading comprehension task. In Group 3, the incidental group, the semantic encoding of the words was also necessary to get a better understanding of the reading passages. With no other assistance, guessing based on the context was the only way for the participants to acquire the meaning of the target words. Therefore, all the three groups achieved improvement in target word acquisition in the post-tests. This result supports Hypothesis 1 and verifies that all the three learning contexts involve deep level of information processing and have a positive effect on target word acquisition.

Findings in this experiment are consistent with the study conducted by Wang (2005). In her study, both the intentional group and the incidental group achieved improvement in target words acquisition after the treatments. However, the reason for the improvement in both learning contexts was not discussed.

Zhang and Wu's (2002) study also proves Craik's claim that information processing on semantic level has a better effect on memory retention than the structural processing. Three groups, Groups 1, 2, and 3, in their study were assigned with different tasks of word learning respectively: One group with intentional learning tasks, one with incidental learning tasks and another with only word form memory tasks. The result shows that both the intentional and incidental learning groups performed better in target word acquisition and retention than the group with only word form memory tasks.

The result is also consistent with the proposal of connectionism. According to connectionism, different concepts are stored in different nodes in the brain, and the memory system is a complicated network of these nodes. The strength of the connection between nodes in the memory system is determined by the correlation between concepts represented by the nodes. New knowledge acquired will be represented by new nodes embedded in the network. Different from the traditional views on knowledge, connectionism emphasizes the importance of the relation between concepts or knowledge. Learning is taken as a process of connecting specialized nodes or information sources. One of the necessary conditions for successful learning is to see the connections between concepts and to nurture and maintain the connections. By connecting new knowledge with old knowledge, the knowledge of the target words presented in the input can be converted into intake and be embedded into the knowledge network in the brain.

The different tasks taken by three experimental groups in this study all involved new and old knowledge that were connected to different extent. For the deductive group, learners connected the meaning of the target words with the context provided in the reading passage and the example sentences. Without the context, the sole L1 equivalences might mislead learners' understanding of the concepts of the target words. For the incidental group and the inductive group, the new word meaning guessing process involved the reading process, which impelled the participants to compare the new knowledge with the old knowledge. The learners could get some clues when they found the connection between the new words and the known words by using both their linguistic knowledge and their background knowledge about the world.

4.4.2 Discussion of Hypothesis 2

Hypothesis 2 predicts that learners receiving the extra inductive information processing or deductive information processing treatment will perform better in target word acquisition and retention than those receiving the incidental learning processing. From the data presented in Table 4-8 and Table 4-13, it can be found that the mean scores of both the inductive and deductive groups on the two VKS post-tests are higher than the incidental group. The results of the one-way ANOVA have further verified that the differences between the inductive group and the incidental group in the mean scores of the two post-tests are at the significant level (p=0.000<0.05). The differences in the mean scores between the deductive group of the two post-tests and the incidental group are also proved to be significant at the 0.05 coefficient level (p=0.000). Moreover, the analysis of the number of target words acquired and retained by each group supports Hypothesis 2a, which predicts that both the inductive and deductive groups will acquire more words than the incidental group. Deeper analysis on the depth of knowledge of the target words also indicates that participants in the two groups involving intentional learning acquired deeper knowledge of the target words than those in the incidental group. Hence, Hypothesis 2b is also supported in this study. Data analysis on the dictation test and the collocation matching test also proves that the inductive or deductive processing treatment has a better effect on acquisition of structural and collocational aspects of word knowledge than the incidental learning treatment.

The results show that the two learning contexts which involved extra information processing have a better effect on new words acquisition and retention than the incidental contest. There are several reasons behind this finding. First, attention is a critical factor which affects the different effects of the intentional and incidental learning contexts on L2 vocabulary learning. The role that attention plays in language learning has been discussed by many researchers (VanPatten, 1996; Schmidt, 2001). They assume that attention is a prerequisite for learning to take place. In VanPatten's Input Processing Model, the critical factor for language acquisition is not input but the transformation process in which input can be converted into intake. Intake refers to form-meaning connections of linguistic data. The form-meaning connections can take place only when input is comprehensible and given sufficient attention by learners. He also indicates that the processing capacities humans possess are limited. In Gass's (1997) Model of SLA, she also attaches great importance to the role of attention in the SLA process. She argues that apperception is the first stage of acquisition. Although input is fundamental for language acquisition, only the input which is perceived by learners has the chance to be comprehended and become intake. Schmidt (1995, 2001) also proposes that the linguistic features exposed to learners can be acquired and are significant only if they are consciously noticed by learners.

For the incidental group, learners paid most of their attention to capturing the meaning of the text. Only the words which would affect comprehension of the text would attract learners' attention, and the ones which would not affect comprehension of the text would be ignored by learners. Moreover, learners used many strategies such as the context and the background knowledge to compensate for their lack of target word knowledge and to obtain the main idea of the text. Hence, learners probably comprehended the text and finished the comprehension tasks without knowing some of the target words. Since learners totally ignored the forms of these unperceived target words, it seemed to be impossible to construct the form-meaning connection of the linguistic items and convert the input into intake. This gives a sound account of why the mean number of the target words acquired by the incidental group was less than the other two groups.

For the target words which had been noticed by learners in the incidental group, only the lexical aspect of the target word knowledge was processed by learners. In the Input Processing Model, VanPatten has proposed that learners tend to direct their attention to certain parts of the input, especially those immediately relevant to the message content, such as the meaning of the content words. For learners in the incidental group, the main purpose of reading the text was to get the main idea of the text and finish the reading comprehension task. They were apt to direct their attention to the semantic aspect of the target words and ignore other aspects. In contrast, to achieve better performance in the word test, the participants in the inductive and deductive groups paid specific attention to other aspects of the target words besides the semantic aspect, such as the orthographic and syntactic aspects of the target word knowledge. The tasks designed for the inductive group and the supplementary information of the target words provided in the word list in the deductive group also intentionally drew learners' attention to other aspects of the word knowledge, such as morphological, grammatical and collocational aspects. The specific attention paid to these aspects of the target words facilitated learners to achieve comprehensive acquisition of the target word knowledge. This was a sound explanation of why depth of target word knowledge acquired by the two intentional groups was better than that acquired by the incidental group.

Second, the deductive and inductive groups have taken more comprehensive elaboration of the target words to transfer input into intake. In VanPatten's (1996) Model of SLA and Gass's (1997) Model of SLA, both of them emphasize the great importance of the transformation process from input into intake. VanPatten (1996) holds that although the acquisition begins with exposure to input, only part of input which is made form-meaning connections by learners can be converted into intake. The intake then will be stored in the working memory and has the potential to be internalized. It is emphasized that SLA depends on intake rather then input, since only intake data is usable for acquisition. Although Gass's (1997) Model of SLA is different from VanPatten's model to some extent, she also places emphasis on the essentiality of the transformation process from input into intake. According to Gass's model, the transformation process is divided into three stages. The input should firstly be perceived by the learners, then comprehended, and the comprehended input finally becomes the intake, which will be integrated into learners' representation system. According to Gass, apperception is not abundant for language acquisition, and input must be comprehended to become intake. She believes comprehension of input entails analyzing the input to extract meaning.

Meaning-extraction is taken as a crucial part in the transformation process from input to intake in both VanPatten (1996) and Gass's (1997) models of SLA. However, for the specific feature of vocabulary, sole meaning-extraction is not sufficient for successful L2 vocabulary acquisition. With the development of research on vocabulary knowledge, knowing a word has never just meant knowing the conceptual meaning of a word. Many researchers (Nation, 1990; Laufer, 1998; Laufer & Paribakht, 1998; Wesche & Paribakht, 1996) propose the concept of depth of word knowledge includes many lexical dimensions. Richard (1976) first proposes the multi-dimension characterization of word knowledge. Nation (1990) further categorizes the word knowledge into four levels or dimensions such as form, position, function and meaning. Therefore, thorough comprehension of input in vocabulary acquisition means achieving a comprehensive understanding of a word in various dimensions.

In Craik's Levels of Processing Model, he proposes that the encoding on multiple dimensions of a linguistic item can achieve a better retention effect than encoding on only one or two dimension. The comprehensive processing of a target linguistic item can leave deeper traces in one's working memory and gain a better effect on language acquisition. Craik's argument supports the concept of multi-dimension comprehension in vocabulary acquisition.

The previous data analyses shown in Table 4-24 have proved that learners in the inductive and deductive groups performed better in the dictation test and the collocational matching test than those in the incidental group. As to the learners in the incidental group, they mainly encoded the target words on the semantic aspect to facilitate comprehension of the reading passages. The other lexical dimensions of the word knowledge which would not affect the reading comprehension would be ignored. Therefore, the other lexical aspects such as the form or grammatical features of the target words were not encoded sufficiently by learners in the incidental group.

In contrast, learners in the inductive and deductive learning groups were given more chances to do more encoding on the form and grammatical aspects of the target words. The fore-warning of the word test directed learners' attention to the formal aspect of target words. In the inductive group, learners were encouraged to analyze the morphological features of the target words, such as the roots and affixes of the target words. In the deductive group, although learners did not receive special instruction on the morphological feature analysis of the target words, many of them copied the written form of the target words to facilitate their memorization. Both of the two groups did more encoding on the form dimension of the target words than the incidental group. With the example sentences provided in the word list, learners in the inductive group and deductive group had more chances to encode the grammatical aspect of the target words.

Third, the effect of the sentence-level textual enhancement also made contribution to the better performance of the inductive and deductive groups. Textual enhancement refers to drawing learners' attention to a particular linguistic item in a text by using typographical cues such as bolding and italics. Although only a few studies on the evaluation of the effectiveness of textual enhancement on improving language learning have been conducted, most of the results in these studies prove the method to be effective (Shook, 1994; Alanen, 1995; Wong, 2002). Only one study conducted by Overstreet (1998) shows the negative effect of textual enhancement on language learning. Tense, relative pronouns, grammatical morphemes, and other grammatical linguistic items are used as target learning items in these studies. There have been only few studies on the effect of textual enhancement on vocabulary learning.

In the present study, the target words were printed in bold in the example sentences for the inductive and deductive groups; while there was no textual enhancement in the reading passages read by the incidental group. The result shows that the textual enhancement did attract learners' attention to the target words and facilitated the vocabulary learning process. Moreover, according to Wong's (2002) study, the sentence-level input was more effective than the discourse-level input. Learners in the inductive and deductive groups had more concentrative processing on the target words than those in the incidental group with only discourse-level input.

In summary, attention, multi-faceted encoding on the target word knowledge and textual enhancement jointly contributed to the better performance by two intentional groups in target words learning and retention.

4.4.3 Discussion of Hypothesis 3

Hypothesis 3 predicts that learners receiving the inductive information processing treatment will perform better on target words acquisition and retention than learners receiving the deductive information processing treatment. This hypothesis is only partially supported by the results of a battery of data analysis. The analysis of the overall gains by the two groups indicates that the mean score of the inductive group in the two post-tests is higher than the deductive group. The results of the one-way ANOVA have further verified that the differences in the mean scores of the two post-tests between the inductive group and deductive group are at the significant level ($p=0.000<0.05$). The differences in the mean scores of the two post-tests between the deductive group and the incidental group are also proved to be significant at the 0.05 coefficient level ($p=0.000<0.05$). It suggests that the inductive group performed better in the overall gains and retention of the target words than the deductive group. However, the comparison of target word acquisition between the two groups in breadth and depth of knowledge aspect are inconsistent. On the one hand, the analysis of the number of target words acquired and retained by each group presents no significant difference. It seems that the inductive processing is no more effective than the deductive processing in increasing the vocabulary size. Hence, Hypothesis 3a, which predicts that the inductive group will acquire more words than the deductive group, is not supported by the results. On the other hand, the further analysis of the frequency distribution of 5 scoring categories in the VKS tests indicates that the vocabulary knowledge acquired by the inductive group is greater in depth than that by the deductive group. Since Category 5 can only be given when a word is used with semantic appropriateness and grammatical accuracy, the larger percentage of the distribution of Category 5 by the inductive group suggests that participants in this group acquired better vocabulary knowledge of the semantic, grammatical and functional aspects than the deductive group.

Results of the two supplementary tests which assess the form and collocational aspects of vocabulary level knowledge do not support Hypothesis 3b. The comparison of the scores in the dictation test indicates that the inductive treatment is no more effective than the deductive treatment in improving the acquisition of form aspect word knowledge. But the comparison of scores in the collocation matching test between the two groups suggest that the inductive treatment is more effective in facilitating the acquisition of collocation aspect of word knowledge.

The results prove that the inductive learning method has a better effect on the L2 vocabulary acquisition than the deductive learning method. Learners in the inductive group gained more vocabulary knowledge in depth. This result is consistent with the findings from Sun's (2006) study, in which the comparison of the relative effects of traditional teaching method and data-driven learning method on L2 vocabulary acquisition was conducted. The findings of this study can be explained from the following perspectives.

Firstly, different task demands involving different cognitive modes affect the effectiveness of L2 vocabulary acquisition and retention. Schmidt (1990) claims that not all the input has equal value, and only the input which is noticed becomes available for intake and effective processing. Noticing, then, is taken as a necessary condition for effective processing. Task demand is considered as one of the important variables affecting noticing (Schmidt, 1990). A particular language task may make certain language forms or linguistic items salient by means of specific task design. Many researchers and instructors have tried to draw learners' attention to target linguistic items by using specific tasks. Fotos and Ellis (1991) deliberately design tasks which focus on adverb placement in the hope that specific task requirements can draw learners' attention to this grammar point. Tarone (1985) also reports a study in which the direct object pronoun use was highlighted and enhanced by a narrative task.

In the present study, different task modes were involved in the two experimental groups. The task used in the inductive group, which mainly involved the inductive cognitive mode, was example-based and required the bottom-up processing. None of the related multiple aspects of the target word knowledge were provided to the learners. Learners were required to complete the blank filling task by generalizing various facets of word knowledge from the main text and the example sentences. In contrast, the task used in the deductive group was more rule-based and required the top-down processing. The multiple facets of knowledge of each target word were directly provided in the word list. The two types of cognitive modes lead to two distinctive teaching and learning methods in the SLA research area. The deductive treatment in the present study is similar to a wide range of traditional language teaching methodologies based on the concept of explicit rule-based system. These teaching methods usually rely on the explicit rule-presentation and play the roles of consciousness-raising and consolidating the target rules or linguistic items. This type of teaching method, which advocates explicit rule presentation, is teacher-centered and has the risk of ignoring the individual features of learners. The explicit rule-based teaching method has caused debate on its effectiveness for a long time. Reber (1989) proposes that the earlier that explicit instruction is provided in training, the better for language learning, In contrast, Mathews et al. (1989) have different views on effective learning, arguing that an explicit model could only be generated based on implicit knowledge.

Unlike the deductive teaching method, the inductive-mode-based task is more learner-centered. Learners are considered not as a knowledge receiver but a knowledge explorer who can actively analysis the language materials and generalize the rules or extract specific linguistic knowledge from the materials by using various strategies. This type of learning method follows the bottom-up order by which the grammatical rules or multiple facets of word knowledge are not presented but induced from the input exposure. The inductive learning method can also find theoretical support from constructivism. The constructivists believe that learning is not a mechanical process of stimulus and response. It is an active process which requires learners to construct their own conceptual structures through reflection and abstraction. Thus, the goal of instruction is not to improve skills or behaviors, but to develop concepts and deep understanding of the selected information. According to Bruner's (1983) theory, the learning method which encourages learners to extract meaning or rules from the input exposure by themselves can greatly enhance their learning motivation and interest. Moreover, it is also beneficial for the intake and long-term store of the learned knowledge. The knowledge learned by rote is difficult to be retrieved.

In the inductive learning method, the role of the instructor in the learning process is also different from that in the traditional learning context. In a traditional learning context, the instructor often dominates the class and is responsible for presenting and illustrating all the word knowledge or grammatical rules. In contrast, the instructor in the inductive learning context is mainly to draw learners' attention to the target words or grammatical rules and help them construct the conceptual structures of the target linguistic items. The instructor is not the dominator of the learning process. Instead, learners take most of the responsibilities for knowledge extraction and construction. This view on the role of the instructor has been supported by many researchers (Schmidt, 1994; Ellis, 1994). Ellis (1994) argues that the function of explicit instruction is to channel attention in selective and beneficial ways and make the words or rules salient in the input materials. Moreover, the instructor in the inductive learning context needs to provide learners with feedback on their hypotheses or generalization of the knowledge.

In the present study, the word knowledge acquired by learners in the inductive group was greater than that of the deductive group. A detailed investigation into the frequency distribution of the 5 scoring categories in the VKS tests reveals that the scores of a great portion of the words by the deductive group are distributed over Categories 3 and 4. It implies that many learners in the deductive group just acquired the meaning aspect of word knowledge. Many errors in the collocation aspect were found in the sentences made by learners in the deductive group. For instance, many learners made wrong collocation with one of the target words *impair*, such as *the earthquake has impaired many buildings*. The word *impair* often collocates with words representing abstract concepts, such as *right*, *mobility*, *view*, *sight* or *health*. These errors may be due to learners' limited understanding of the concept of *impair*. Learners simply viewed *impair* as an equivalent of *damage*. They failed to realize the collocation constrains of the word and mixed its use with *damage*, which could collocate with both concrete words and abstract words. In contrast, learners in the inductive group extracted the features of the words that collocated with the word *impair* from a series of example sentences under the instructor's instruction. Hence, few similar errors were found in the sentences made by learners in the inductive group.

In addition, the different input presentation modes lead to different degrees of saliency, which affect the effectiveness of input processing. According to Schmidt (1990), perceptual saliency is one of the important factors which can influence the input-intake transition process. The saliency concerns how prominent a target linguistic item or grammatical point can be noticed in the input. The more salient an item is, the more likely it is to be acquired. Correspondingly, the less prominent it is, the less likely it is to be acquired.

The usual way for enhancing the perceptual saliency of a target linguistic item is to visually change its printing mode, such as printing it in bold, italic or underlining it. However, the specific features of vocabulary make the saliency promotion method for a word quite different from that for a grammatical item. As reviewed in the former sections, vocabulary acquisition involves the learning of multiple facets of word knowledge. It seems to be difficult to make all these dimensions of knowledge salient by just printing the word in bold. Hence, another input enhancing method was developed in the present study to improve the saliency of various aspects of word knowledge. The author tried to design a new way of presentation to make the multiple facets of word knowledge emerge. In the inductive group, the information of the target words was not directly presented in the word list. In the word list, each target word was followed by three example sentences. In addition, some blanks and brackets in which the specific facets of word knowledge such as morphological features, conceptual meaning, association, grammatical features and collocation were required to be filled in. In fact, the word list could actually be regarded as a word journal in which learners were required to write down the multiple facets of the target word knowledge through learning and assistance provided by the instructor. These blanks and brackets forced learners to pay their attention to the specific dimensions of the target word knowledge and to notice the gap between the old information and unknown information.

As to the deductive group, although the multiple facets of vocabulary knowledge were saliently presented in the word list, it was difficult to ensure all the information of the target word knowledge would be noticed and encoded equally by the learners. In the informal interview with some participants in the deductive group reported that they tended to pay more attention to the spelling and meaning of the target words instead of the grammatical and functional aspects. This could explain why many participants in this group used the target words in wrong forms or grammatical categories when they were required to make sentences in the VKS test. For instance, some students used *standstill* as a verb in the sentence *Finally we made the car standstilled.* Some gave a wrong inflection of a word in a sentence like *The fog dispersed as quickly as it gathered.* Fewer similar errors were found in the sentences made by the learners in the inductive group in the VKS test.

4.4.4 Factors affecting input processing in L2 vocabulary acquisition

According to the discussion on the three hypotheses, several factors which may affect the effectiveness of input processing in L2 vocabulary acquisition can be identified as follows. Firstly, different task demands based on different cognitive modes will impact the transition process from input into intake. The inductive tasks which encourage learners to extract or generalize the multiple facets of word knowledge from the linguistic instances have a better effect on L2 vocabulary acquisition and retention than the traditional rule-based learning tasks. In contrast with the explicit knowledge presentation, the inductive learning tasks are more learner-centered and provide learners with more opportunities to construct their own conceptual structure from the input exposure by using various strategies. The process of analyzing and encoding can direct their attention to the gap between old knowledge and new knowledge, and deepen their understanding of various aspects of word knowledge. The inductive learning method can promote learners' motivation and autonomy in learning. In contrast, the traditional rule-based instruction may be less effective in facilitating the L2 vocabulary acquisition. Knowledge acquired through mechanic memorizing may stay at a superficial level and is not effective for long-term storage and retrieval.

Secondly, depth of elaboration may also affect the effectiveness of input processing in L2 vocabulary acquisition. Input encoding on the semantic level is believed to be deeper than the structural level encoding. Besides, the contrast between the two groups with extra information processing and the incidental group proves that encoding on multiple dimensions of a linguistic item could achieve a better retention effect than encoding on only one or two dimensions. The comprehensive processing of a target linguistic item could leave deeper traces in one's language developmental system.

Thirdly, the different input presentation modes may also affect the effects of vocabulary acquisition. The contrast between the test performances of the inductive group and the incidental group in the present study suggests that the sentence-level input is more effective than the discourse-level input. The discourse-level input seems to be too time-consuming for vocabulary learning, and the long interval between the repeated appearances of a word is not good for the knowledge transition from short-term to long-term storage system. In contrast, the sentence level seems to be more efficient in enhancing the frequency of target words in a short time. The rich and authentic linguistic context may also facilitate encoding of a word in various contexts. Moreover, the distinct characteristic of vocabulary knowledge requires new ways of input presentation. A common textual enhancement such as highlighting the target word is far from efficient to channel learners' attention to multiple dimensions of word knowledge. The word journal paper used in the inductive group seems to be more effective in directing learners' attention to different aspects of word knowledge than the traditional word list mode. In contrast with the traditional word list, which directly presents the knowledge of a target word in the list, the blanks and brackets in the word journal paper force learners to extract the knowledge of target words by themselves.

4.5 Summary

The experimental study illustrated in this chapter compared three vocabulary learning contexts based on various input processing modes. Three different scoring methods were used to give dimensional interpretation of the performances of participants in the VKS tests. Firstly, the comparison of the overall gains for the four groups suggests that all the three types of treatments, the inductive type, deductive type, and incidental type, had positive effects on facilitating L2 vocabulary acquisition. Among the three experimental groups, the inductive group performed the best in the two post VKS tests, followed by the deductive group. The incidental learning context was the least effective in improving L2 vocabulary acquisition and retention among the three types of learning contexts. Secondly, the comparison of the numbers of target words acquired and retained by the three groups indicates that all the three groups made some progress in vocabulary increase. Both the inductive group and the deductive group acquired and retained more words than the incidental group. However, although the results of one-way ANOVA indicate a significant difference between the inductive group and deductive group in number of words, the inductive group actually just gained one more word than the deductive group and the difference between the two groups was not so great. Thirdly, the contrast of the frequency distribution of 5 scoring categories between groups suggests that the inductive group gained the most word knowledge in depth among the three experimental groups, followed by the deductive group. Few scores of the incidental group distributed in Categories 4 and 5, which implies that word knowledge acquired by this group only reached a shallow level and they failed to use the words correctly and appropriately in sentences. In a word, all the interpretations of the performances in VKS tests from different perspectives suggest that the inductive input processing method is the most effective in facilitating L2 vocabulary acquisition, especially in improving the word knowledge in depth.

Factors affecting the input processing effects in L2 vocabulary acquisition are also discussed based on the findings in the experiment. The different task demands based on specific cognitive modes may greatly affect the effectiveness of input encoding in the L2 vocabulary learning process. The inductive type of cognition mode is suggested to be more effective than the deductive mode in which the word knowledge or grammatical rules are explicitly presented to learners. The inductive mode is learner-centered and provides learners with chances to extract knowledge and deepen their understanding of the knowledge by themselves. It can also improve learners' motivation and autonomy in the learning process. Knowledge acquired through this method is easier to be stored in the long-term memory. Depth of input elaboration is another important factor in the input encoding process. The more elaborately a linguistic item is encoded, the longer it will be stored in one's language development system. The comprehensive encoding of multiple facets of the word knowledge will greatly enhance the input-intake transition. Another factor which may affect L2 vocabulary acquisition is the role of the instructor in the learning process. The traditional teaching method which simply presents the vocabulary knowledge or grammatical rules to learners seems to be ineffective in enhancing the L2 acquisition and retention. The instructor needs to change the traditional concept of instruction and find ways to draw learners' attention to the words and accumulate various aspects of word knowledge by themselves. Last but not least, results in the study suggest that the sentence-level input is more efficient than the discourse-level input in enhancing word appearance frequency and vocabulary acquisition and retention.

Chapter 5 An empirical study on output processing in L2 vocabulary acquisition

5.1 Introduction

This experiment was conducted for two purposes: To investigate the roles of output in L2 vocabulary acquisition, and to explore the co-effect of input and output processing on L2 vocabulary acquisition. Through the comparative study, the relative effects of three task modes with different cognitive loads (input processing task, output processing task, and input plus output processing task) were evaluated to find out which task mode could best enhance the L2 vocabulary acquisition. This chapter will begin with a brief description of the research design, research questions and hypotheses of this experiment. Then, the procedures of the experiment, such as the participants, different task modes, and task procedures will be introduced in detail. Since the experimental materials and test instruments adopted in Experiment 2 were the same as those in Experiment 1, no more description will be given on these two parts. Based on the data obtained from the experiment, the experimental results will be reported and discussed in terms of relevant theories and previous experimental findings. Both the roles and limitations of output in L2 vocabulary acquisition generalized from the findings of this study will also be discussed in the latter part of this chapter. Last but not least, pedagogical implications drawn from the findings will be given, and the optimal instructional contexts for vocabulary learning will be suggested at the end of this chapter.

5.2 Method

5.2.1 Research design and hypotheses

The role of input processing in L2 vocabulary acquisition has been discussed in the previous chapter. Since output is also an important part in the information processing flow, the goal of this experiment was to explore the role of output in L2 vocabulary acquisition and to compare the relative effects of three task modes on L2 vocabulary acquisition. As discussed in Chapter 3, many researchers have acknowledged that solely input processing is far from sufficient for L2 learning. They also have emphasized the critical role output plays in L2 vocabulary acquisition (Skehan, 2000; Swain, 1995). They believe that output is not only the product of language development, but also the practice process, which performs several functions to facilitate language development (Swain, 2005; Pica, 1994; Van den Branden, 1997). It is suggested that the production of target linguistic items can help learners notice the gap between their interlanguage and the target language, and testify their hypotheses on the target linguistic items. As to L2 vocabulary acquisition, it is suggested that output can help learners to notice the form of the target words, deepen the semantic elaboration, enhance the retrieval speed, and strengthen the retention of target words (Kwon, 2006). The production of target words in context can also facilitate the transfer of receptive word knowledge into productive word knowledge, and enhance the automaticity of word use. However, some comparison studies on instructions with or without output processing indicate that output processing seems to have no unique effect on L2 vocabulary acquisition (Izumi et al., 2000; Liu, 2006).

Although the role of output in SLA has been confirmed in many theories, results of empirical studies on the effect of output on L2 vocabulary acquisition are still inconclusive. On the one hand, the effects of different output instruction modes on L2 vocabulary acquisition are debated by L2 vocabulary researchers and instructors. Some empirical studies have proved that the semantic-oriented output activities, such as translation and sentence composing, can enhance the acquisition of new words (Coomber et al., 1986; Prince, 1996). It is also suggested that writing on a topic related to the reading materials provides learners with opportunities to use the words contextually. On the other hand, even the effect of output on facilitating L2 vocabulary acquisition is still questioned by some researchers. It is suggested that the output tasks may have no positive effect or even inhibit L2 vocabulary acquisition (Barcroft, 2000, 2004).

Moreover, it is also important to note that the advocacy of the critical role of output in L2 vocabulary acquisition may easily lead to another extreme, which is to overemphasize the importance of output and ignore the role of input in L2 vocabulary acquisition. Ellis and He (1999) argue in their study that the positive effect of output on word learning cannot occur without the previous input encoding process.

Based on these reviews, Experiment 2 was conducted to answer the following research questions and testify the following hypotheses:

1) Does output have a positive effect on L2 vocabulary acquisition?

2) What are the relative effects of input elaboration plus output instruction and output-only instruction on L2 vocabulary acquisition?

3) Does the input-plus-output vocabulary instruction have the best effect on enhancing L2 vocabulary acquisition among the three approaches?

Hypothesis 1: The comprehensive treatment (input processing + output task) will perform a better effect on L2 vocabulary acquisition than the input processing treatment (input processing only).

Hypothesis 1a: Learners in the comprehensive group (input processing + output task) will gain more words than those in the input processing group (input processing only).

Hypothesis 1b: Learners in the comprehensive group (input processing + output task) will gain greater depth of word knowledge than those in the input processing group (input processing only).

Hypothesis 2: The comprehensive treatment (input processing + output task) will have a better effect on L2 vocabulary acquisition than the output processing treatment (output task only).

Hypothesis 2a: Learners in the comprehensive group (input processing + output task) will gain more words than those in the output processing group (output processing only).

Hypothesis 2b: Learners in the comprehensive group (input processing + output task) will gain greater depth of word knowledge than those in the output processing group (output processing only).

Hypothesis 3: The comprehensive treatment will achieve the best effect on L2 vocabulary acquisition among the three treatments.

5.2.2 Subjects

120 participants, aged from 18 to 20, took part in this experiment. All of these participants were freshmen of non-English majors from three parallel classes in Shanghai Normal University. They were enrolled in the university after the National Matriculation English Test. Before the administration of the experiment, they had comprehensive English courses for non-English majors for four weeks. At the beginning, 124 students took part in the pre-tests for measuring their average English proficiency and vocabulary level; however, during the treatment conducting and post-testing process, 4 students in total were absent from the treatment procedures or the delayed post-test. Therefore, only 120 participants' data were available for the

current study. Three classes were randomly divided into four groups: 31 in the comprehensive group, 30 in the output only group, 30 in the input only group, and 29 in the control group.

All the participants in these groups were considered to have similar levels of English proficiency. However, to ensure that there were no significant differences in English proficiency among the four groups, one-way ANOVA was conducted to compare all students' scores in the entrance English examination, which was conducted before the beginning of the term. As shown in Table 5-1 and Table 5-2, the average scores of the four groups are similar.

Table 5-1 Mean scores of the English proficiency test for the four groups

Group	*N*	Minimum	Maximum	Mean	Std. deviation
1	31	63.00	97.00	83.1452	9.2504
2	30	60.00	98.00	82.4194	9.8616
3	30	62.00	97.00	81.9356	9.1625
4	29	65.00	96.00	82.7333	8.0855

Note: 1= comprehensive group, 2= output only group, 3= input only group, 4= control group

Table 5-2 One-way ANOVA of the mean scores of the English proficiency test

Group	Sum of squares	*df*	Mean square	*F*	Sig.
Between groups	30.276	3	10.092	0.120	0.948
Within groups	9716.091	116	83.759		
Total	9746.367	119			

The VLT (Nation, 1990) was administered to check whether there were significant differences among the four groups in terms of their vocabulary knowledge. The participants' scores on each level of the VLT and on the VLT as a whole were analyzed by using one-way ANOVA. The results shown in Table 5-3 indicate that participants in the four groups had no significant differences in both the overall vocabulary size and each word frequency level.

Table 5-3 Comparison of the mean scores in the VLT for the four groups

	Group 1		Group 2		Group 3		Group 4		ANOVA	
Subtest	*M*	*SD*	*M*	*SD*	*M*	*SD*	*M*	*SD*	*M*	*SD*
2000	15.55	1.61	15.23	2.53	15.68	1.47	16.09	2.36	0.214	0.808
3000	12.84	3.73	12.63	2.43	11.43	2.96	12.30	3.12	1.820	0.168
5000	6.16	2.59	6.86	3.12	5.23	3.56	6.08	3.15	2.072	0.132
University	5.62	2.33	5.23	2.07	5.75	4.16	5.12	2.96	0.014	0.986
10,000	3.35	1.19	2.90	1.60	2.76	1.38	3.01	1.41	1.480	0.866
Overall	43.25	8.27	42.86	7.89	40.10	9.72	42.08	8.68	1.194	0.308

Note: 1= comprehensive group, 2= output only group, 3= input only group, 4= control group

5.2.3 Task modes

This is a quasi-experimental study with a pre-test and post-test design involving three treatment groups and one control group. Different task modes were involved in the three treatment groups respectively. The details related to the four groups will be introduced in the following part.

The output only group involved only output processing treatment. Learners in this group were required to do a reconstruction task (See Appendix F) based on the reading text without any previous input encoding and instruction on the target words. The meaning of the target words was directly given to the learners. Evidence of the previous empirical studies suggests that writing on the topic related to the reading materials will impulse learners to use the target words contextually (Verhallen & Schoonen, 1998). Using new words in the writing task can draw learners' attention to the form of the target words. Using the words in sentence or discourse context can also deepen their encoding on various aspects of the target word knowledge. The reconstruction task based on the original text provides learners with more time to restructure and monitor their use of interlanguage than the oral modality.

Learners in the input only group were also asked to read the same reading text at the beginning of the treatment. Instead of doing the reconstruction task, learners in the input only group were asked to do the inductive type of word knowledge processing task, which was the same as the task used in the inductive group in Experiment 1. The meaning of the target words and other aspects of word knowledge were not provided and must be inferred by learners from the reading materials and example sentences. The instructor provided learners with corrective feedback when they generated incorrect guessing. However, learners in the input processing group were given no opportunities to use the target word contextually.

The comprehensive group involved both input and output processing tasks. Learners in this group firstly elaborated encoding on the target words through the provided materials. After input encoding, learners were required to do the reconstruction task to use the words contextually as the same as learners in the output group.

The control group involved neither explicit input instruction nor output processing. Learners in this group were just required to read Reading Passage One and do the reading comprehension task. No specific input or output processing task was involved in this group.

5.2.4 Task procedures

The study was conducted in the following four stages:

1. Pre-test: A vocabulary knowledge test for target words was administered before the treatment started. 12 target words mixed with other 14 non-target words were also tested to find whether participants had some knowledge of the target words. 14 non-target words were used to distract learners' attention from the target words and eliminate the memory effect on the coming study.

2. Treatment conducting: The treatments for the four groups were conducted two weeks later in their normal class time after the conduction of the pre-tests. First, all the four groups were given 10 minutes to read

Reading Passage One. Then, the four groups received different treatments. Participants in Group 1, the comprehensive group, were given both the input processing treatment and the reconstruction task. The input processing treatment was the same as that used in the inductive group in Experiment 1. They were required to generalize various aspects of word knowledge from the example sentences through guessing and analyzing with elicitation and assistance from the instructor. The wrong inference or generalization on the word knowledge would be corrected by the instructor. Then, the reading materials and word lists were collected, and participants were assigned with the text reconstruction task. To lessen the memory load of the content of the text, participants were provided with some sentences in the original text as a cue for the structure of the text. Chinese equivalents of the target words were also provided to lessen participants' workload of obtaining the meaning and use of the target words in context (see Appendix F).

As for Group 2, the input only group, participants received the input processing treatment, which was the same as learners did in the comprehensive group. No reconstruction task was involved in this group. Conversely, participants in Group 3, the output only group, were directly assigned with the reconstruction task after reading the passage. No word elaboration instruction was involved in this group. Participants in Group 4, the control group, were required to do the corresponding reading comprehension questions. No explicit input or output vocabulary instruction was involved. Moreover, participants were not forewarned about the target word test after the treatment.

3. Immediate post-test: Once the treatments were finished, all the experimental materials and note papers were collected and an immediate post-test was administered to compare the effectiveness of different treatments on acquisition of the 12 target words. The VKS test was used in this test.

4. Delayed post-test: Two weeks after the immediate post-test, the same test was taken again to investigate the relative effect on word retention of different treatments.

5.3 Results

5.3.1 Results of the overall vocabulary gains

A series of statistical analyses were conducted to answer the research questions in this experiment: 1) whether participants in each group made significant progress in the VKS test over time; and 2) whether there were significant differences in the VKS test performance among groups after receiving different treatments. Therefore, two independent variables and one dependent variable were involved in this experiment. One of the independent variables was time factor, including three levels (the pre-test, immediate post-test, and delayed post-test). The other independent variable was the task mode, which included input plus output processing, output only processing, input only processing, and text exposure without elaborated processing. The dependent variable is the vocabulary knowledge test on the target words. Mean scores of different groups over time for the vocabulary knowledge test were firstly compared to examine the effect of the independent variables. One-way ANOVA was done to verify the significant differences between groups for each time and between different times for each group.

5.3.1.1 Comparison of scores on the pre-test of VKS for the four groups

The VKS test was used in both the pre-test and two post tests to measure the gains of word knowledge before and after different treatments. Each word was measured on a scale from 1 to 5 points. Since 12 target words were used in this experiment, the possible total score for 12 words ranged from 12 to 60.

Table 5-4 shows that the mean scores in the pre-test of the four groups are all close to the lowest score boundary 12, suggesting that the participants were quite unfamiliar with most of the target words and failed to provide the meaning of these words. Moreover, there seems no obvious difference in the mean scores between groups. The results of further one-way ANOVA shown in Table 5-5 indicates that there are no significant differences in the mean scores of the pre-test between groups (p=0.113>0.05).

Table 5-4 Descriptive statistics on the pre-test of the VKS for the four groups

Group	*N*	Minimum	Maximum	Mean	*Std. deviation*
Group 1	31	12.00	15.00	13.5161	1.36311
Group 2	30	12.00	16.00	15.2667	1.31131
Group 3	30	12.00	16.00	13.1333	1.22428
Group 4	29	12.00	17.00	14.0345	1.26725

Note: 1= comprehensive group, 2= input only group, 3=output only group, 4= control group

Table 5-5 One-way ANOVA of the pre-test of VKS for the four groups

Group	Sum of squares	*df*	Mean square	*F*	Sig.
Between Groups	23.045	3	7.682	4.586	0.113
Within Groups	189.263	116	1.675		
Total	212.308	119			

5.3.1.2 Comparison of scores on the immediate post-test between groups

5.3.1.2.1 Comparative results of the pre-test and the immediate post-test of VKS for each group

Data shown in Table 5-6 suggest that mean scores in the immediate post-test by all the four groups have increased to different extent from those in the pre-test. The results of paired sample t tests presented in Table 5-7 verify the significance of the increases by each group. It implies that all three experimental groups made significant improvement in their VKS performance after the treatment (comprehensive group: t= -79.671, p=0.000<0.05; input only group: t= -37.487, p=0.000<0.05; output only group: t= -21.487. p=0.000<0.05).

Table 5-6 Descriptive statistics on the immediate post-test of VKS for the four groups

Group	*N*	Minimum	Maximum	Mean	Std. deviation
1	31	48.00	60.00	55.7097	3.14318
2	30	28.00	54.00	48.1000	6.74741
3	30	36.00	59.00	42.7000	5.01962
4	29	24.00	33.00	27.5862	2.65272

Note: 1= comprehensive group, 2= input only group, 3=output only group, 4= control group

Table 5-7 Paired sample *t* test between the pre-test and the immediate post-test for each group

Group		Paired differences					*t*	*df*	Sig. (2-tailed)
		Mean	Std. deviation	Std. error mean	95% confidence interval of the difference				
					Lower	Upper			
1	Pre-test/ post test 1	-5.21935E1	2.94866	0.52960	-43.27513	-41.11197	-79.671	30	0.000
2	Pre-test/ post test 1	-3.49667E1	5.10904	0.93278	-36.87441	-33.05892	-37.487	29	0.000
3	Pre-test/ post test 1	-2.84333E1	7.24775	1.32325	-31.13969	-25.72698	-21.487	29	0.000
4	Pre-test/ post test 1	-1.389E1	2.99219	0.55564	-15.03472	-12.75838	-25.010	28	0.000

Note: 1= comprehensive group, 2= input only group, 3=output only group, 4= control group

5.3.1.2.2 Comparison of scores on the immediate post-test of VKS between groups

Results in Table 5-8 indicate that the mean scores of three empirical groups in the immediate post-test were all higher than those of the control group. It suggests that all the three empirical groups gained more vocabulary knowledge than the control group. Among the three empirical groups, the mean score of the comprehensive group was much higher than those of the input only group and the output only group. It indicates that the comprehensive group performed best in the immediate post-test, followed by the input only group and the output only group.

Table 5-8 Gains in the pre-test and the immediate post-test of VKS for each group

Group	Pre-test	Post-test 1	Gain 1
1	13.5161	55.7097	42.1936
2	13.1333	48.1000	34.9667
3	15.2667	42.7000	28.4333
4	14.0345	27.5862	13.5571

Note: 1= comprehensive group, 2= input only group, 3=output only group, 4= control group

Figure 5-1 gives a clearer illustration of the comparison of the gains after the treatment by the four groups. It can be found from Figure 5-1 that the comprehensive group gained more vocabulary knowledge after the treatment than the input only group and the output only group. One-way ANOVA was conducted to further verify whether there were significant differences in the immediate post-test performance between the comprehensive group and the input only group, and between the comprehensive group and the output only group.

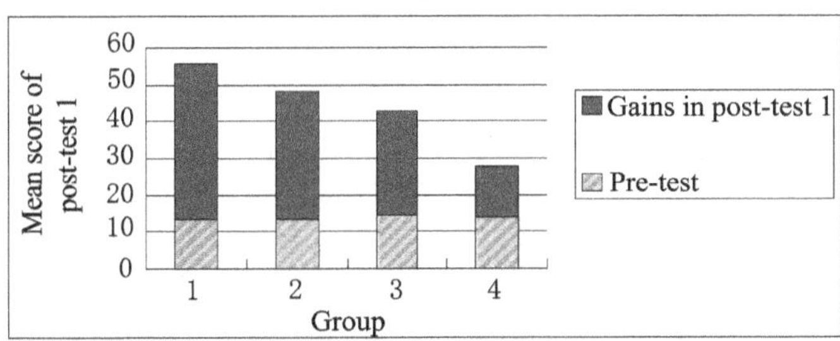

Figure 5-1 Comparison of gains in the pre-test and the immediate post-test of VKS for each group

Results in Table 5-9 indicate that there were significant differences between groups. Data shown in Table 5-10 give a more detailed verification of the significance of the difference in the immediate post-test between groups. It can be found that the mean scores of three experimental groups, Groups 1, 2 and 3, are all significantly different from that in the control group, Group 4. The result of comparison between Group 1 (the comprehensive group) and Group 2 (the input only group) proves that there is a significant difference between the mean scores of the two groups (p=0.000<0.05). It implies that the input plus output treatment has a better effect on L2 vocabulary learning than the input only treatment. Thus, Hypothesis 1 is supported. The result of the comparison between Group 1 and Group 3 indicates that the mean scores of the two groups are significantly different (p=0.000<0.05). It supports Hypothesis 2 which predicts that the input plus output treatment is more effective in facilitating L2 vocabulary acquisition than the output only treatment.

Table 5-9 One-way ANOVA of the immediate post-test of VKS for the four groups

Group	Sum of squares	*df*	Mean square	*F*	Sig.
Between groups	12290.743	3	4096.914	189.095	0.000
Within groups	2513.249	116	21.666		
Total	14803.992	119			

Table 5-10 Multiple comparisons of mean scores in immediate post-test of VKS for the four groups

Group		Mean difference	Std. error	Sig.	95% confidence interval	
					Lower bound	Upper bound
1	2	13.00968*	1.19210	0.000	9.6277	16.3916
	3	7.60968*	1.19210	0.000	5.2277	10.9916
	4	27.77864*	1.20250	0.000	25.3672	31.1901
2	1	−13.00968*	1.19210	0.000	−16.3916	−9.6277
	3	−5.40000*	1.20183	0.000	−8.8096	−1.9904
	4	14.76897*	1.21215	0.000	11.3301	18.2078
3	1	−7.60968*	1.19210	0.000	−10.9916	−5.2277
	2	5.40000*	1.20183	0.000	1.9904	8.8096
	4	20.16897*	1.21215	0.000	16.7301	23.6078
4	1	−27.77864*	1.20250	0.000	−31.1901	−25.3672
	2	−14.76897*	1.21215	0.000	−18.2078	−11.3301
	3	−20.16897*	1.21215	0.000	−23.6078	−16.7301

*. The mean difference is significant at the 0.05 level.

Note: 1= comprehensive group, 2= input only group, 3=output only group, 4= control group

5.3.1.3 Comparison of mean scores on the delayed post-test for the four groups

5.3.1.3.1 Comparative results of the pre-test and the delayed post-test of VKS for each group

One week later after the treatment, participants in the four groups were given the delayed post-test without prior notice. The delayed post-test, which also used the VKS test to test participants' knowledge of the 12 target words, was conducted to investigate how much the knowledge of the 12 target words participants was retained after a one-week interval. The descriptive data shown in Table 5-11 suggest that participants in each group retained much target word knowledge to different extent. Paired sample t tests were conducted to verify whether there was a significant difference in retention of the target word knowledge compared with the performance in the pre-test (Table 5-12).

Table 5-11 Descriptive statistics on the delayed post-test for the four groups

Group	*N*	Minimum	Maximum	Mean	Std. deviation
1	31	41.00	59.00	49.1290	5.47021
2	30	30.00	48.00	43.1000	5.30196
3	30	30.00	50.00	40.2667	5.78901
4	29	20.00	29.00	24.6897	1.98393

Note: 1= comprehensive group, 2= input only group, 3=output only group, 4= control group

Table 5-12 Paired sample t test between the pre-test and the delayed post-test of VKS for the four groups

Group		Paired differences					*t*	*df*	Sig. (2-tailed)
		Mean	*Std. deviation*	Std. error mean	95% confidence interval of the difference				
					Lower	Upper			
1	Pre-test / post-test 2	−3.56129E1	4.86948	0.87458	−37.39904	−33.82676	−40.720	30	0.000
2	Pre-test / post-test 2	−2.996E1	5.34292	0.79290	−31.58834	−28.34500	−37.794	29	0.000

Continued

Group		Paired differences					*t*	*df*	Sig. (2-tailed)
		Mean	*Std. deviation*	Std. error mean	95% confidence interval of the difference				
					Lower	Upper			
3	Pre-test / post-test 2	−2.400E1	6.18675	1.12954	−26.31017	−21.68983	−21.248	29	0.000
4	Pre-test / post-test 2	−1.065E1	2.53935	0.47154	−11.62109	−9.68926	−22.596	28	0.000

Note: 1= comprehensive group, 2= input only group, 3=output only group, 4= control group; Post-test 2= delayed post-test

Results of the paired sample *t* test shown in Table 5-12 indicate that there was a significant difference between the pre-test and the delayed post-test for each group. It suggests that all the three experimental groups had retention of the acquired target word knowledge to some extent. These findings imply that all the three treatments had positive effects on the retention of the acquired word knowledge. Although all the three treatments were proved to have positive effects on word knowledge retention, the degree of effectiveness for each group was still not clear. To obtain the details on the difference in effectiveness of the three experimental groups, comparison of the retention of word knowledge between groups will be conducted in the next section.

5.3.1.3.2 Comparison of scores in the delayed post-test of VKS between groups

Data shown in Table 5-13 indicate that participants in the three experimental groups all made some retention of the acquired target word knowledge. Figure 5-2 presents a clearer illustration of the different amount of retention by the four groups. It can be found from that the comprehensive group had the most retention of the acquired word knowledge in the delayed post-test, followed by the input only group. The output only group had the least retention of the knowledge of target words. One-way ANOVA was conducted to further verify whether there were significant differences in the effectiveness of word knowledge retention between groups.

Table 5-13 Gains in the immediate post-test of VKS for the four groups

Group	Pre-test	Post-test 2	Gain 2
1	13.5161	49.1290	35.6129
2	13.1333	43.1000	29.9667
3	15.2667	40.2667	26.0000
4	14.0345	24.6897	10.6552

Note: 1= comprehensive group, 2= input only group, 3=output only group, 4= control group, Gain2 = difference gap between post-test 2 and pre-test

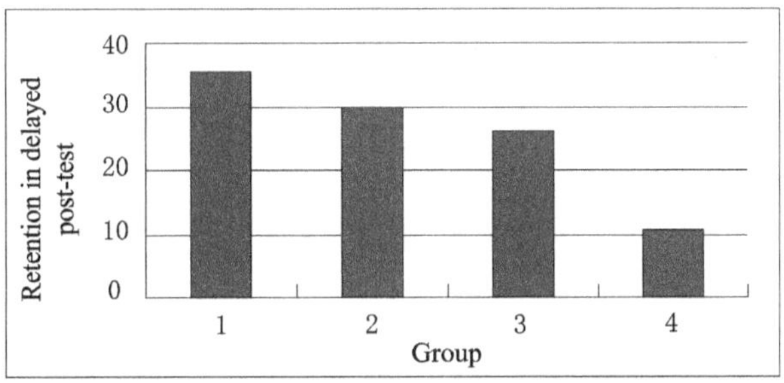

Figure 5-2 Comparison of gains in the delayed post-test for the four groups

Note: 1= comprehensive group, 2= input only group, 3=output only group, 4= control group, Gain2 = difference gap between post-test 2 and pre-test

Results shown in Table 5-15 indicate that the mean scores of all the three experimental groups are significantly higher than that of the control group. It suggests that all the three treatments had positive effects on the retention of the acquired word knowledge. Moreover, the data also reveal significant differences in the effectiveness of word knowledge retention among different experimental groups. The comprehensive group had better retention of word knowledge than the input only group (p=0.000<0.05) and the output only group (p=0.000<0.05).

To sum up, the results of the overall gains in the three VKS tests show a rough comparison of the relative effects of different experimental treatments on L2 vocabulary acquisition. All the three treatments were proved to have a positive effect on the acquisition and retention of the target word knowledge. The input plus output treatment was proved to have the best effect on the acquisition and retention of L2 vocabulary, followed by the input only treatment, and the output treatment.

Table 5-14 One-way ANOVA of the delayed post-test of VKS for the four groups

Group	Sum of squares	*df*	Mean square	*F*	Sig.
Between Groups	9639.743	3	3213.248	168.031	0.000
Within Groups	2218.257	116	19.123		
Total	11858.000	119			

Table 5-15 Multiple comparisons of mean scores of the delayed post-test for the four groups

Group		Mean difference	Std. error	Sig.	95% confidence interval	
					Lower bound	Upper bound
1	2	10.86237*	1.11995	0.000	7.6851	14.0396
	3	6.02903*	1.11995	0.000	2.8517	9.2063
	4	25.43938*	1.12973	0.000	21.2344	27.6444
2	1	−10.86237*	1.11995	0.000	−14.0396	−7.6851
	3	−4.83333*	1.12910	0.001	-8.0366	−1.6301
	4	13.57701*	1.13879	0.000	10.3463	16.8077
3	1	−6.02903*	1.11995	0.000	−9.2063	−2.8517
	2	4.83333*	1.12910	0.001	1.6301	8.0366
	4	18.41034*	1.13879	0.000	15.1796	21.6411
4	1	−25.43938*	1.12973	0.000	−27.6444	−21.2344
	2	−13.57701*	1.13879	0.000	−16.8077	−10.3463
	3	−18.41034*	1.13879	0.000	−21.6411	−15.1796

*: The mean difference is significant at the 0.05 level.

Note: 1= comprehensive group, 2= input only group, 3=output only group, 4= control group

5.3.2 The number of target words acquired and retained

Section 5.2.1 gives a comparison of the general gains shown in the two post VKS tests between groups, but it seems to be too simplified to draw a conclusion from the results of a singular comparison of general gains by each group. To obtain a more comprehensive understanding of the acquisition of the target words by each group, the comparison of the number of the target words acquired and retained by each group was conducted. The method of counting the number of acquired words according to the scores in the VKS test was the same as the one used in the pilot experiment. Hence, the scoring method will not be explained again and the mean number of acquired and retained words by each group will be presented as follows.

The data shown in Table 5-16 indicate that the numbers of words acquired and retained by the three experimental groups were larger than those by the control group. It suggests that participants in the three experimental groups all learned and retained more words than the control group. Figures 5-3 and 5-4 give a more detailed illustration of the differences in the number of words acquired and retained by different experimental groups. It can be found from Figure 5-3 that the comprehensive group learned the most words among the three experimental groups, followed by the input only group and the output only group. The results of comparison on the amount of retained words between groups illustrated in Figure 5-4 are similar. The comprehensive group retained the most words among the three experimental groups, followed by the input only group and output only group. A series of one-way ANOVA were conducted to verify the significance of the differences in the number of acquired words between different groups (Table 5-17).

Table 5-16 Descriptive statistics on the number of words acquired by the four groups in three tests

	Group 1		Group 2		Group 3		Group 4	
Vocabulary test	*M*	*SD*	*M*	*SD*	*M*	*SD*	*M*	*SD*
The pre-test	0.23	0.37	0.36	0.15	0.29	0.31	0.21	0.17
The post-test 1	10.81	2.21	9.27	1.63	8.96	1.25	3.01	1.22
The post-test 2	8.74	2.07	7.37	1.56	7.05	1.39	2.06	1.02

Note: Group 1= comprehensive group, Group 2= input only group, Group 3= output only group, Group 4=control group

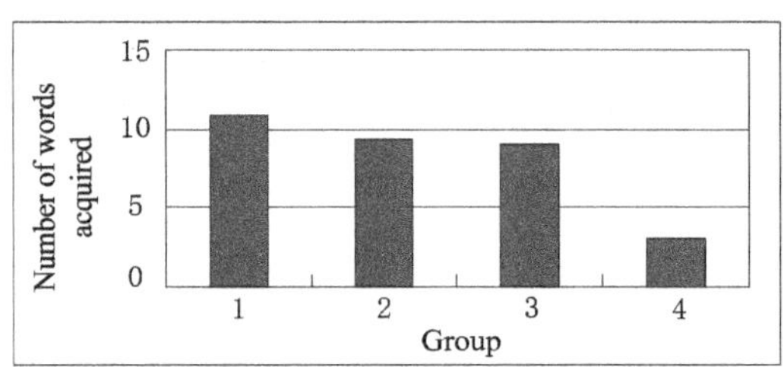

Figure 5-3 Comparison of the number of words acquired by each group

Note: 1= comprehensive group, 2= input only group, 3= output only group, 4=control group

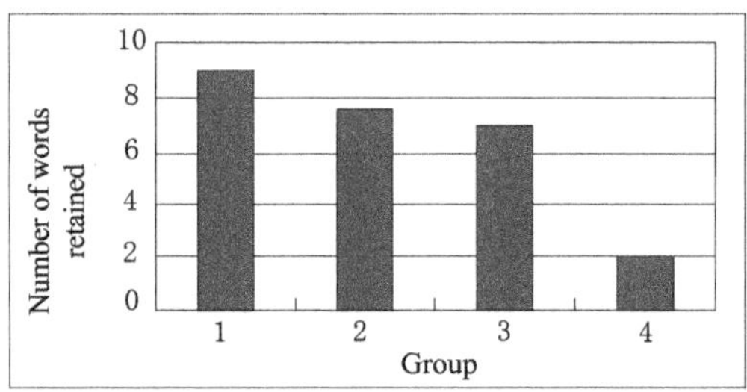

Figure 5-4 Comparison of the number of words retained by each group

Note: Group 1= comprehensive group, Group 2= input only group, Group 3= output only group, Group 4=control group

The data shown in Table 5-18 prove that the number of words acquired by each experimental group is significantly bigger than that by the control group. Hence, Hypothesis 1 which predicts that all the three methods will have positive effects on L2 vocabulary acquisition is proved to be true again. Hypothesis 2 which predicts that the input plus output treatment will have a better effect on L2 vocabulary acquisition than the input only group is also proved to be true ($p = 0.029 < 0.05$). The data also provide positive evidence for the assumption that participants in the comprehensive group will acquire more words than those in the output only group.

Table 5-17 One-way ANOVA of the number of words acquired by the four groups

Group	Sum of squares	*df*	Mean square	*F*	Sig.
Between Groups	915.557	3	305.186	132.469	0.000
Within Groups	267.243	116	2.304		
Total	1182.800	119			

Table 5-18 Multiple comparisons of the mean number of words acquired by the four groups

Group		Mean difference	Std. error	Sig.	95% confidence interval	
					Lower bound	Upper bound
1	2	1.19032*	0.38873	0.029	0.0875	2.2931
	3	1.42366*	0.38873	0.005	0.3208	2.5265
	4	7.18687*	0.39212	0.000	6.0744	8.2993
2	1	−1.19032*	0.38873	0.029	−2.2931	−0.0875
	3	0.23333	0.39190	0.949	−0.8785	1.3452
	4	5.99655*	0.39527	0.000	4.8752	7.1179
3	1	−1.42366*	0.38873	0.005	−2.5265	−0.3208
	2	−0.23333	0.39190	0.949	−1.3452	0.8785
	4	5.76322*	0.39527	0.000	4.6419	6.8846
4	1	−7.18687*	0.39212	0.000	−8.2993	−6.0744
	2	−5.99655*	0.39527	0.000	−7.1179	−4.8752
	3	−5.76322*	0.39527	0.000	−6.8846	−4.6419

Note: *. The mean difference is significant at the 0.05 level.
1= comprehensive group, 2= input only group, 3=output only group, 4= control group

Results of the one-way ANOVA suggest that all the three experimental groups retained more words than the control group. It supports again Hypothesis 1 (Table 5-19). It can also be inferred from the data in Table 5-20 that the number of target words retained by participants in the comprehensive group is significantly larger than that by participants in the input only group (p=0.000<0.05) and the output only group (p=0.000<0.05). It suggests that the input plus output treatment has a better effect on the retention of the acquired L2 vocabulary than both the input only treatment and the output only treatment.

Table 5-19 One-way ANOVA of the number of words retained by the four groups

Group	Sum of squares	*df*	Mean square	*F*	Sig.
Between groups	762.091	3	254.030	184.133	0.000
Within groups	160.034	116	1.380		
Total	922.125	119			

Table 5-20 Multiple comparisons of the mean number of words retained by the four groups

Group		Mean difference	Std. error	Sig.	95% confidence interval	
					Lower bound	Upper bound
1	2	1.53978*	0.30082	0.000	0.6864	2.3932
	3	1.67312*	0.30082	0.000	0.8197	2.5265
	4	6.73749*	0.30344	0.000	5.8766	7.5983
2	1	−1.53978*	0.30082	0.000	−2.3932	−0.6864
	3	0.13333	0.30327	0.979	−0.7270	0.9937
	4	5.19770*	0.30587	0.000	5.3299	6.0655
3	1	−1.67312*	0.30082	0.000	−2.5265	−0.8197
	2	−0.13333	0.30327	0.979	−0.9937	0.7270
	4	5.06437*	0.30587	0.000	4.1966	5.9321
4	1	−6.73749*	0.30344	0.000	−7.5983	−5.8766
	2	−5.19770*	0.30587	0.000	−6.0655	−5.3299
	3	−5.06437*	0.30587	0.000	−5.9321	−4.1966

* The mean difference is significant at the 0.05 level.

Note: 1= comprehensive group, 2= input only group, 3=output only group, 4= control group

To sum up, this section explores the different effects of the three learning methods on new words acquisition. The results provide positive evidence for the hypothesis that all the three types of learning methods have a positive effect on the acquisition and retention of L2 vocabulary. As to Hypothesis 2, the present data have verified the assumption that the input plus output treatment has a better effect on L2 vocabulary acquisition than the input only treatment. Moreover, results of one-way ANOVA have proved the significant difference in the effects on facilitating new words acquisition and retention in terms of quantity between the input plus output treatment and the output only treatment. However, it should be noted that although the differences in the quantitative aspect of word acquisition between the comprehensive group and the other two experimental groups were statistically significant, participants in the comprehensive group averagely acquired and retained only one or two more words than those in the input only or output only group. It suggests that three treatments had similar effects on increasing the L2 vocabulary size.

5.3.3 Comparison of depth of vocabulary knowledge acquired by three experimental groups

The comparison of the number of words acquired and retained by different groups suggests that the three treatments were not varied greatly in their effect on increasing the vocabulary size. However, the way of measuring the number of words acquired and retained failed to distinguish depth of target word knowledge acquired by participants receiving different instructional treatments. Detailed information on the acquisition of depth of target word knowledge by different groups will be illustrated according to the frequency distribution of the 5 scoring categories in the three VKS tests by different groups.

The frequency distribution of the 5 scoring categories in the VKS tests provides more detailed information about depth of word knowledge acquired and retained by different groups. The figures (See Figures 5-5, 5-6, and 5-7) below also present the developmental patterns of depth of word knowledge before and after different treatments. Data shown in Table 5-21 indicate that the scores provided by the four groups are mostly distributed in Category 1 or 2. It suggests that participants in all the four groups had never seen the target words before or had seen before but failed to provide the meaning of these words. In the immediate post-test (See Figure 5-6), all the three groups made improvement in depth of target vocabulary knowledge after different treatments. For the comprehensive group, 78% of the scores are distributed into Category 5. It implies that participants in comprehensive group performed a considerable improvement in depth of their vocabulary knowledge and they could use more than three-quarter of the target words with semantic appropriateness and grammatical accuracy in a sentence. As to the input only group and the output only group, only 60.6% and 52.7% of the scores of words reached Category 5. The contrast between the comprehensive group and the other two experimental groups suggests that participants in the comprehensive group demonstrated the greatest depth of word knowledge compared with those in the other two experimental groups based on their higher percentage of the score distribution in Category 5.

In the delayed post-test (See Figure 5-7), 43.6% of scores of the comprehensive group reach Categories 4 and 5. As to the input only group and the output only group, only 35.2% and 31.6% of scores reach Category 5. It implies that participants in the comprehensive group retained greater depth of knowledge than those in the input only group and the output only group.

Table 5-21 Frequency distribution of 5 scoring categories in the pre- and post- VKS tests

Test	Group	Category 1	Category 2	Category 3	Category 4	Category 5
Pre-test	1	69.4%	29.7%	0.8%	0.1%	—
	2	82.1%	17.4%	0.5%	—	—
	3	78.3%	20.8%	0.9%	—	—
	4	72.9%	26.7%	0.4%	—	—
Immediate post-test	1	—	10.2%	3.4%	7.6%	78.8%
	2	—	22.8%	9.7%	6.9%	60.6%
	3	—	25.3%	10.8%	11.2%	52.7%
	4	21.6%	53.4%	11.6%	8.3%	5.1%
Delayed post-test	1	5.3%	21.9%	9.5%	19.7%	43.6%
	2	8.9%	29.7%	10.3%	15.9%	35.2%
	3	15.4%	25.8%	14.7%	12.5%	31.6%
	4	29.6%	53.2%	7.4%	5.2%	5.6%

Note: 1= comprehensive group, 2= output only group, 3=input only group, 4= control group

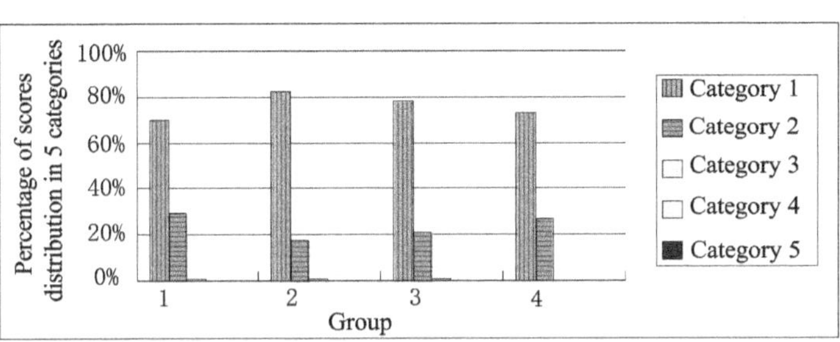

Figure 5-5 Categories distribution in the pre-test for the four groups

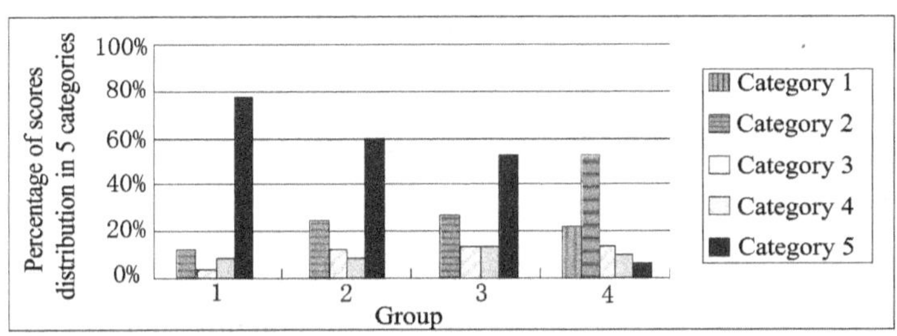

Figure 5-6 Categories distribution in the immediate post-test for the four groups

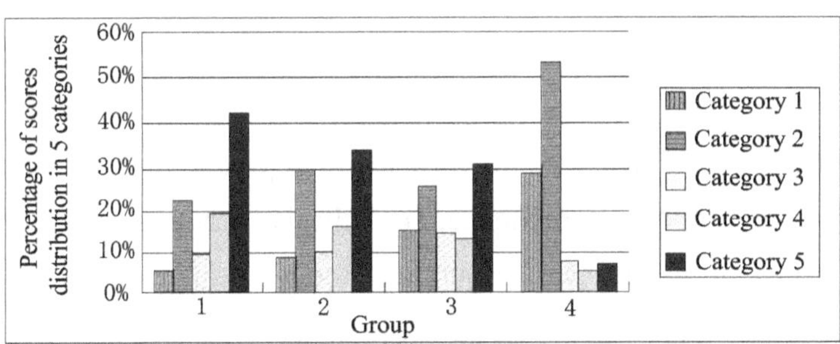

Figure 5-7 Categories distribution in the delayed post-test for the four groups

In summary, a comprehensive comparison of the frequency distribution of the 5 scoring categories for the four groups in three VKS tests implies that the comprehensive group acquired and retained greater depth of word knowledge than the input only group and the output only group. The results also suggest that all the three experimental groups had considerable increases in depth of word knowledge after different treatments.

5.4 Discussion

5.4.1 Discussion of Hypothesis 1

Hypothesis 1 predicts that the input plus output instruction treatment will have a better effect on enhancing L2 vocabulary acquisition than the input only treatment. Three different scoring methods were used to present a comprehensive illustration of the differences between groups in vocabulary acquisition. The comparison of the mean scores between the two groups in the two post VKS tests shows that the mean scores of the comprehensive group in the immediate and the delay post-tests are higher than that of the input only group. Data generated from one-way ANOVA verify that the differences in the mean scores between the output group and the input only group in the two post-tests reach the significant level (p=0.000 <0.05). It implies that the comprehensive group performed better in the overall vocabulary gains than the input only group. The number of words acquired and retained by the two groups were also calculated and compared according to the results of the VKS test. The results show that the number of words acquired and retained by the comprehensive group is significantly larger than that by the input only group. Hence, Hypothesis 1a has been verified. The comparison of the frequency distribution of the 5 scoring categories between the two groups suggests that the output group acquired deeper knowledge of the target words than the input only group. It is found that the percentage of Category 5 for the output only group is much higher than that for the input only group. It indicates that learners receiving the output treatment acquired greater depth of word knowledge at semantic and grammatical levels. Moreover, the larger amount of distribution in Category 5 implies that the output task can greatly enhance learners' productive knowledge.

The results are consistent with Hulstijn and Trompetter's (1998) study, which proves that words used in a composition with the L1-L2 dictionary available are better retained than those encountered in an input processing task. A study by Ellis and He (1999) also suggests that the modified output task is more effective than the input task. It is suggested that writing tasks can provide learners with more opportunities to process the target vocabulary in depth in a short period of time, since time is an important issue in L2 learning and instruction context.

However, the results are inconsistent with Liu's study (2006) in which the output group fails to outperform the contrast group receiving no output treatment in new words acquisition. The different findings from two studies may be due to the vocabulary testing measurement. The vocabulary test used in Liu's study is asking learners to give the correct form of the target words with their L1 equivalents. It should be noted that this type of testing instrument can only assess the form aspect of the word knowledge and can give no information about whether other aspects of word knowledge have been acquired or not. However, the roles of output in L2 vocabulary acquisition are far more than drawing learners' attention to the formal aspect of vocabulary and enhancing the word form acquisition. Output also provides learners with the opportunity to notice other aspects of the word knowledge such as meaning, grammatical patterns and appropriateness. Learners can test their hypotheses and deepen their understanding of the depth of word knowledge in the process of production. The context-independent testing mode fails to assess learners' ability to use the words in context. Moreover, the productive knowledge of the target words which may be enhanced in the production process can not be assessed according to the results in the testing instrument. In this sense, the results of the blank-filling test used in Liu's study only present the comparison of two groups in acquiring the form aspect of word knowledge. It seems to be too simple to draw a conclusion from the performance in only one dimension of word knowledge.

In contrast, the VKS test gives a clear illustration of learners' word knowledge acquisition process, from knowing the receptive knowledge (Categories 1 and 2) to acquiring the productive knowledge (Categories 3, 4 and 5), and from knowing the single aspect of word knowledge to obtaining multiple facets of word knowledge. It can be found from the results of the VKS test that the output treatment has a better effect on improving the receptive-to-productive word knowledge transition than the input only learning treatment. It also proves that depth of knowledge acquired by learners receiving the output treatment is greater than that of learners without the output treatment.

There are several reasons for the outperformance of the comprehensive group.

Firstly, the production task used in the comprehensive group involved more cognitive load, which can greatly enhance depth of elaboration than the input only group. According to Hulstijn and Laufer's (2001) Involvement Load Hypothesis, the more cognitive load involved in a task, the more elaborated and deeper a word will be processed and then the better it will be acquired. In the framework of psycho-cognitive theory, many researchers have given detailed analysis to the cognitive load involved in different task processing modes (Hulstijn & Laufer, 2001; Zhang and Wu, 2003). It is suggested that retrieving lexical information from memory and putting it to use take the most involvement load, followed by processing the noticed information. Noticing information about words is considered as taking the least involvement load among the three cognitive dimensions. In this sense, the production task involves more cognition load than the input processing task and may promote learners to make more elaborated encoding on the vocabulary. In the present study, learners in the comprehensive group were asked to reconstruct the reading text with the assistance of content clues. In this sense, learners in the output group made much deeper elaboration of the target word knowledge than the input group.

Moreover, the deep elaboration or processing involved in the output tasks not only improved the word learning process but also facilitated the retention of the acquired word knowledge. It has been widely acknowledged in the cognitive psychology research field that retention of information depends on the quantity and quality of cognition that a learner devotes to multiple facets of words. Word knowledge retention can also be enhanced by associating new information with existing information in both quantitative and qualitative aspects. It is also argued that the output condition itself can improve depth of elaboration than the input condition due to the linguistic complexity such as semantic, morphological and grammatical processing involved in the production task (Swain, 1995). These arguments support the findings in the present study. In Experiment 2, learners in the comprehensive group performed better in retention of the acquired words than the input only group in both the quantitative and qualitative aspects of word knowledge. This finding is consistent with the conclusions drawn from other similar studies (Nobuyoshi & Ellis, 1993; Hulstijn & Trompetter, 1998; Ellis & He, 1999; Hulstijn & Laufer, 2001). Findings drawn from these studies suggest that words used in production tasks can be better retained than words practiced in non-production tasks.

Secondly, the output task provided learners with opportunities to test their hypotheses on the understanding of the target words and notice the gap between their interlanguage and the target language. According to Swain's (1995) claims in the Output Hypothesis, learners acquire L2 vocabulary by forming hypotheses on the target linguistic items and then testing them out based on external feedback from their output. Moreover, it is argued by Swain that learners can try out new vocabulary or other linguistic items even if external feedback is not available for modification or reproduction of their output. Meanwhile, learners are forced to use their metalinguistic knowledge to monitor their output before and after the output process. It can greatly enhance the internalization of their production of language. In the present study, instead of the Chinese translation of the whole sentence, the clues provided were only L1 equivalents of target words and other keywords necessary for the reconstruction. Thus, special attention should be paid to the syntactical and semantic aspects of word knowledge during the reconstruction process. Learners needed to use their metalinguistic knowledge to monitor their production in the process of completing the reconstruction task. It offered learners with more chances to internalize the vocabulary knowledge into their developmental system of L2.

Thirdly, the reconstruction task used in the comprehensive group pushed learners to improve their productive aspect of word knowledge. According to Schmitt and Read's (2001) definition of different levels of word knowledge, the word knowledge development ranges from receptive knowledge, which refers to recognition of a word, to productive knowledge, which refers to using the word with grammatical and semantic accuracy in a sentence. However, in the learning process from receptive to productive knowledge, word comprehension does not automatically lead to correct production of words. Learners often do not use a word correctly or retrieve it freely for production even if they can recognize it. It is argued that the gap between receptive and productive knowledge of vocabulary is due to learners' inadequate control over words. The meaning of 'control' in this sense means how fast and freely a learner can retrieve the information which is stored in various dimension of the lexicon such as the semantic, syntactic and functional knowledge of a word. It is suggested that learners are less likely to notice their lack of target vocabulary knowledge until they are forced to produce it. In this sense, output plays a crucial role in drawing learners' attention to target vocabulary knowledge and impelling them to reduce the gap between their receptive and productive vocabulary knowledge.

In the present study, learners in the comprehensive group were required to rewrite the reading text by using all the target words. In the course of reconstruction, the productive knowledge of the target words could be enhanced. In contrast, learners in the input only group were more concerned with comprehending the word knowledge extracted from the input exposure. Learners in the input only group just acquired the receptive knowledge of the target words. Since they were not required to use the word in context, they had no need and motivation to learn the productive aspect of word knowledge. The result is consistent with Webb's (2007) study in which he also finds that learners doing comprehension practice do not perform as well as those doing sentence composing practice in the productive word knowledge test.

5.4.2 Discussion of Hypothesis 2

Hypothesis 2 predicts that the input elaboration plus output treatment will have a better effect on enhancing L2 vocabulary acquisition than the output only treatment. Results gained from different scoring methods of learners' performance in VKS tests give interpretation to the relative effects of two treatments on L2 vocabulary acquisition from different perspectives.

The results of the overall gains in the two post VKS tests indicate that the mean scores of learners in the comprehensive group are higher than the output group. Further, the one-way ANOVA proves the significant differences in mean scores between the two groups (p=0.000 < 0.05). It suggests that the comprehensive group performed better than the output group in the overall vocabulary gains. Results of the comparison of the number of words acquired and retained between the two groups show that learners in the comprehensive group gained more words than those in the output group. The data of the frequency distribution of 5 scoring categories indicate that the percentage of distribution in Categories 4 and 5 in the comprehensive group is higher than that of the output group. It suggests that learners in the comprehensive group had greater gains in depth of target word knowledge. The results of VKS tests from different perspectives all prove that the input plus output treatment has a better effect on L2 vocabulary acquisition and retention both in breadth and depth aspects.

It can be drawn from these findings that the collaborative treatment of input elaboration and production has a better effect on L2 vocabulary acquisition than that of a single output treatment. Although production is quite important for enhancing L2 vocabulary acquisition, especially in the productive aspect, the simple use of target words in context cannot be very effective in improving vocabulary acquisition and retention without necessary previous understanding of word knowledge. In the informal interview of learners in the output group conducted after the immediate post-test, some of them reported that it seemed to be difficult for them to directly use the words in the reconstruction tasks since the L1 equivalents of the target words failed to provide other aspects of the word knowledge, such as the collocation and syntactic knowledge. Although they had learned some knowledge of the new words through using them in the context, they were still not very confident in making sentences by using some of the target words in the post VKS tests. The in-depth observation of sentences made in the VKS tests by the output group reveals that most sentences were quite similar or even the same as those in the reconstruction task in the content or structure aspect. In contrast, sentences made by learners in the comprehensive group in the VKS tests were more diversified in content and structure.

The main reason which may account for the outperformance of the comprehensive group in the VKS tests is that the input plus output treatment provided learners with more input exposure and deeper elaboration of the target word knowledge than the output treatment. The example sentences used at the input processing stage provided learners with the use of target words in various contexts. Learners could extract more aspects of word knowledge from the examples such as different collocations, the subtle differences in the use of a target word in different registers or linguistic contexts. The inductive input processing also provided learners with more opportunities to make deeper elaboration or encoding of the target word knowledge from various aspects. This result is consistent with Kwon's (2006) findings in her study of comparison on relative effects of different learning conditions on L2 vocabulary acquisition. It is reported in her study that the collaboration of input and output treatments can greatly enhance the acquisition and retention of target word knowledge. In Ellis and He's (1999) study, they also indicate that the production treatment will not be effective without necessary input elaboration, and it seems to be difficult to clearly distinguish between the effects of input processing and production on L2 vocabulary acquisition. Special attention needs to be paid to the distinction of effects on visual input enhancement and input elaboration on enhancing the acquisition of word knowledge. Some studies prove that there seems to be no obvious difference between the co-effect of textual input enhancement plus production and single effect of production treatment on L2 vocabulary acquisition (Song, 2008). It should be noted that the visual input enhancement can just facilitate the apperception of the form of a target word and cannot necessarily ensure deep elaboration on the target word knowledge from diverse facets such as semantic, grammatical or functional aspects. The ineffectiveness of such a type of collaborative treatment is due to the superficial and insufficient elaboration of the input. It implies that deep-level encoding of the input materials may maximize the co-effect of input processing and production on L2 vocabulary acquisition.

The input elaboration and production are two inevitable stages in the information processing flow, and the conduction of one may facilitate the effectiveness of the other. The sufficient elaboration of the input facilitates learners to form their hypotheses on the target word knowledge or other linguistic items. Conversely, the production tasks provide learners with opportunities to test their hypotheses on the target word knowledge by means of using the word in context. The positive or negative feedback of the hypothesis may help learners reconstruct their understanding of the target words and enhance the transition process from comprehended input into intake.

5.5 Roles of output in L2 vocabulary acquisition

Summarizing the discussion on the two hypotheses in Experiment 2, the roles of output in L2 vocabulary acquisition can be generalized into three aspects, i.e. cognitive involvement load, hypothesis testing and word knowledge conversion from receptive to productive knowledge.

Firstly, the production tasks involve more cognitive load which can enhance depth of elaboration of the target words. Among the various cognitive dimensions, the cognitive dimension in the production tasks involves the highest cognitive load, which requires the retrieval of the lexical information and put it into use in context. The more cognitive load involved, the deeper a target word will be elaborated or encoded. Many aspects of word knowledge can be elaborated in much greater depth and it is beneficial for the transition of input into intake. Moreover, the deep encoding of the target words may leave a deeper trace of the word knowledge in learners' memory and can facilitate both the long-term store and retrieval of the target word knowledge.

Secondly, the output task provides learners with opportunities to test their hypotheses on the target word knowledge and notice the gap between their interlanguage and the target language. Compared with the input processing tasks, which just require the recognition of the meaning or other aspects of word knowledge in a certain context, the production tasks also push learners to use the word syntactically in a sentence. In the course of production, the gap between their interlanguage and the target language will be found. Learners may pay special attention to certain aspects of word knowledge that they lack, and deepen their understanding of the word knowledge based on external or internal feedback. However, it should be noted that the noticing triggering function of output is not always so effective in every aspect of the word knowledge. The grammatical aspect of word knowledge may easily be ignored because many learners are apt to pay more attention to the semantic aspect of word knowledge and do not find their production to be problematic in the grammatical aspect in the output tasks.

Thirdly, output can enhance the conversion of word knowledge from receptive knowledge into productive knowledge. In contrast with the comprehension tasks which can enhance the receptive knowledge of a word, the production tasks may provide learners with more opportunities to use it in actual context and to test their hypotheses on target words. The automaticity and accuracy of word use will be greatly enhanced with the output practice and corresponding external and internal feedbacks.

5.6 Limitations of output processing in L2 vocabulary acquisition

Although the output tasks can greatly enhance the acquisition and retention of word knowledge, it should be noted that the solely output treatment is far from enough for L2 vocabulary acquisition. The output treatment seems to be not so effective in some aspects of vocabulary acquisition.

Firstly, it is not always effective in drawing learners' attention to every aspect of knowledge. Some learners may consider that they do not have problems with grammatical forms and are apt to ignore the feedback on the grammatical form of the target words.

Secondly, insufficient input exposure to the target words used in various contexts may confine learners' understanding of the words to a limited depth. Learners can only form their hypotheses on the target word knowledge based on the information of the words used in one or two instances. The other specific meanings or collocations of a word used in different contexts or registers cannot be obtained. When learners are required to use the words in context, they are apt to copy the syntactic structures they have seen form the input material.

5.7 Co-effect of input and output processing in L2 vocabulary acquisition

The above analysis on the limitation of roles of output in L2 vocabulary acquisition reminds us that successful L2 vocabulary acquisition can only be achieved by means of the co-effect of elaborated input and output processing. The input and output processing are two important stages in the information processing flow, and they closely correlate with each other. The lack of one will affect the effectiveness of the other on L2 vocabulary acquisition. Sufficient and elaborated encoding of the input can provide learners with more information about the target words, deepen their understanding of word knowledge, and make the production process much easier. Conversely, despite the result of the input processing, the production process is also part of the learning process. It promotes hypotheses testing, facilitates the word knowledge retention and retrieval, and improves the transition from receptive into productive knowledge.

5.8 Summary

Experiment 2 described in this chapter aimed to explore the roles and limitations of output in L2 vocabulary acquisition. The co-effects of input and output processing were also investigated in this experiment. Three experimental groups, the output only group with the reconstruction task, the input only group with the input processing task, and the comprehensive group with both input processing and reconstruction task, were compared to find the best way of enhancing L2 vocabulary acquisition. Three types of scoring methods were used to give a comprehensive interpretation of learners' performance in the VKS tests from multiple perspectives. The results indicate that learners receiving the reconstruction treatment gained greater depth of word knowledge than those without. Learners receiving both input and output processing treatments gained the greatest depth of word knowledge among the three experimental groups. According to the findings from the present study, the roles of output in L2 vocabulary acquisition include in-depth elaboration, hypothesis-testing and receptive-to-productive knowledge conversion. Possible limitations of output in vocabulary acquisition were also discussed. One limitation is that output might not always be effective in promoting the grammatical aspects of knowledge since some learners' overconfidence in their grammatical knowledge inhibits them from noticing the feedback on their errors in grammatical forms. The other limitation of output may be that the effectiveness of output might decrease if lacking necessary and sufficient input processing of the target word knowledge before output. Findings drawn from this study suggest that the input processing and output processing of word knowledge are two necessary stages in L2 vocabulary acquisition, and the joint work of the two variables is the optimal way of enhancing acquisition and retention of L2 vocabulary.

Chapter 6 Conclusion

6.1 Introduction

This chapter summarizes the major findings of two experiments, and the contributions of the research, including theoretical and methodological significance. Pedagogical implications drawn from the findings of the experiments will also be discussed. At the end of this chapter, the limitations of the research and recommendations for further research will be addressed in the hope of shedding some light on the further study in this field.

6.2 Major findings

The main purpose of this study was to investigate the L2 vocabulary teaching and learning process from the cognitive perspective. It is believed that the vocabulary learning follows the similar way to the information processing flow, which consists of both input and output processing stages. Guided by this conception, two experiments were conducted to explore the best way of enhancing the L2 vocabulary acquisition and constructing a cognitive-oriented L2 vocabulary learning model.

Experiment 1 aimed to compare the relative effects of three learning contexts based on distinctive cognitive modes on enhancing input elaboration and input-to-intake transition. The findings of Experiment 1 are as follows:

1) All the three input processing modes (the inductive mode, the

deductive mode, and the incidental mode) had positive effects on enhancing both breadth and depth of word knowledge. The results from the VKS tests demonstrate that both breadth and depth of word knowledge of all the three groups had increased after the treatments.

2) The two intentional learning contexts with extra sentence-level input processing (the inductive mode and the deductive mode) had a better effect on L2 vocabulary acquisition and retention than the incidental learning context. Learners in the two intentional groups gained more words and greater depth of word knowledge than those in the incidental group. Results of two supplementary word tests also reveal that learners in the two intentional groups performed better than those in the incidental group on acquisition of form and collocation aspects of word knowledge.

3) The inductive mode was more effective in enhancing L2 vocabulary acquisition than the deductive mode. The inductive type of cognitive mode was learner-centered, and it encouraged learners to construct their own concepts of the word knowledge under the teacher's guidance. This type of problem-solving task was effective in promoting learners' motivation and autonomy. It could also greatly facilitate the long-term memory of the acquired word knowledge. In contrast, the deductive group which were directly presented with the multiple facets of target word knowledge were more rule-based and in line with the top-down type of cognitive mode. It was more teacher-centered and was not as effective as the inductive type of learning method on L2 vocabulary acquisition and retention.

4) Input presentation might have an impact on the effectiveness of L2 vocabulary acquisition. The sentence-level input was more effective than the discourse-level input on facilitating L2 vocabulary acquisition. Results in this research indicate that the sentence-level input could greatly increase the new word exposure frequency in a limited time interval. Various linguistic contexts provided by the sentence-level input helped learners to

make comprehensive encoding of different dimensions of word knowledge, such as form, meaning, collocation and function. In contrast, learners in the incidental learning context may solely process the semantic aspect of target word knowledge to obtain better comprehension of the text. Other aspects of word knowledge which may not affect comprehension were easily ignored. Target words which may not affect understanding of the passage would even be totally neglected by the learners.

Experiment 2 was conducted for the following three purposes. Firstly, the roles of output in L2 vocabulary acquisition were explored by comparing the relative effects of instructions with or without output tasks on new word acquisition. Secondly, the relative effects of the comprehensive treatment and output treatment on word acquisition were contrasted to find the limitations of output in L2 vocabulary acquisition. Thirdly, the effectiveness of three learning conditions was compared to develop an optimal cognitive model for L2 vocabulary acquisition. Findings drawn from this experiment are as follows:

1) Output is not just the result of learning but plays critical roles in the learning process. The roles of output in L2 vocabulary acquisition lie in the following aspects.

Firstly, output processing involved much cognition involvement load, and could greatly improve the long-term retention and retrieval of the acquired word knowledge. Secondly, it provides learners with more opportunities to test their hypotheses on the target words, and facilitates the input-to-intake transition process. Last but not least, the transition of target word knowledge from receptive knowledge into productive knowledge can also be promoted by production.

2) Although output processing is of vital importance for vocabulary learning, it was found in this research that output still had its limitations in promoting L2 vocabulary acquisition. Output seemed to be inefficient in promoting some aspects of word knowledge, especially in grammatical forms

of a word. It was mainly due to learners' overconfidence in their knowledge of grammatical form. Some learners were apt to ignore the feedback on their grammatical errors since they believed they did not have problems in their grammatical knowledge.

3) Input and output processing are two important stages for L2 vocabulary acquisition. The lack of any stage would reduce the effectiveness of the other on L2 vocabulary acquisition. Sufficient and elaborated encoding of the input could help learners to deepen their understanding of word knowledge, and enhance their confidence in production. Conversely, the lack of sufficient input exposure and encoding could make learners feel unconfident in word using. They could avoid making original sentences and confine their sentence production to simple syntactic structures or limited linguistic contexts. Thus, learners could hardly benefit from output through hypotheses formulation and testing.

6.3 Contributions of the book

6.3.1 Theoretical significance

The present research aims at studying L2 vocabulary acquisition from a cognitive perspective. It is a tentative study and is of theoretical importance. The major theoretical significance lies in the following aspects.

Firstly, this research investigates the L2 vocabulary acquisition within Skehan's (1998) information processing framework. The critical role of cognition in L2 learning has been confirmed by SLA researchers (Skehan, 1998; VanPatten, 1990; Schmidt, 1990; Gass, 1985, 1995; Robinson, 2001). Many researchers attempt to conduct their SLA research from a cognitive perspective, in the hope of developing new L2 learning models which are more concordant with the cognitive rules of language learning (Izumi, 2001;

Vinther, 2005; Robinson & Ha, 1993; Swain & Lapkin, 1995; McLaughlin, 1990; VanPatten & Cadierno, 1993; Doughty, 1991; Ge, 2006; Song, 2007). However, a general review of related literature reveals that most of the cognitive-based SLA studies focus on the investigation of grammar learning (White, 1989, 1990; Swain, 1998; VanPatten, 1993; Schmidt, 1993; Loschky & Bley-Vroman, 1993). Although L2 vocabulary learning has attracted many researchers' attention, few studies have been conducted to explore the cognitive modes involved in L2 vocabulary acquisition. It seems to be difficult to find a systematic theoretical framework in SLA for L2 vocabulary acquisition research. Till now, many studies have been confined to contrasting relative effects of different instructional methods, such as intentional learning and incidental learning. Few studies have given interpretation of L2 vocabulary learning development from a cognitive perspective (Kwon, 2006; Liu, 2006; Sun, 2006; Song, 2008).

Secondly, this research explores the joint effect of input and output processing and constructs a L2 vocabulary acquisition model from a cognitive perspective. Most previous studies on cognitive-based L2 vocabulary acquisition focus on only one stage of information processing, such as input or output processing. The author of this study believes that the L2 vocabulary acquisition process should be regarded as an entire information processing flow which consists of input exposure, input processing and output processing. The overemphasis solely on the effect of any stage in the flow may lead to the neglect of the roles other stages play in the vocabulary learning process. It is suggested in the present research that an optimal L2 vocabulary acquisition model consists of the inductive type of input processing and output processing.

Thirdly, this research probes into cognitive modes in different learning contexts, which are often ignored by many researchers. The rule-based deductive mode and exemplar-based inductive mode are two different types of cognitive modes in the learning process. The rule-based top-down deductive mode emphasizes the explicit presentation of grammatical rules or linguistic items. In contrast, the exemplar-based bottom-up inductive mode stresses more the implicit generalization of linguistic rules through instances exposure. Comparison of effects of the two cognitive modes have been mainly conducted in the field of grammatical knowledge learning, but only a few studies have been done in the vocabulary learning area. It is found in this research that the inductive mode can efficiently promote learners' learning motivation and autonomy and is effective in promoting L2 word knowledge acquisition. This proposal confirms the position of constructivists who hold that learning is an active knowledge construction process which greatly depends on learners' own mental processing.

Fourthly, this research also collects and summarizes factors that may impact input processing during the vocabulary learning process and enrich the present theoretical system of L2 vocabulary acquisition. Factors affecting input processing in grammatical knowledge learning have been widely investigated in previous studies (VanPatten, 1994, 1996; Slobin, 1973; Robinson, 1996). However, only a few studies are associated with exploring the factors which may impact on input processing in L2 vocabulary acquisition. Among these limited studies, most studies focus on investigating the beneficial conditions for incidental learning or studying the effects of involvement load in word learning. Input processing is rarely studied apart from other word learning phases or variables. This study attempts to give a relatively comprehensive summary of factors that may affect input processing in L2 vocabulary learning. The cognitive mode, the depth of elaboration, and the textual enhancement mode are suggested to be the three major factors which may affect the performance of input processing and input-to-intake transition in L2 vocabulary acquisition process.

Last but not least, this research gives an explanation of the roles and limitations of output in L2 vocabulary acquisition based on Swain's (1995)

Output Hypothesis. It also testifies the significance of Output Hypothesis in L2 vocabulary acquisition research field. In Swain's Output Hypothesis, functions of output in SLA have been systematically and comprehensively instructed. Functions proposed by Swain are the general roles of output in the entire SLA field. Roles of output probably vary in different specific linguistic areas such as grammar and vocabulary. The function of output in one area may not be necessarily effective in another. After viewing the specific characteristics of vocabulary learning, the roles of output in L2 word learning are generalized in this study.

6.3.2 Methodological significance

In addition to the theoretical significance which contributes to the study of L2 vocabulary acquisition, this research is also of methodological significance, which enriches the assessment of the depth of vocabulary knowledge. The methodological significance of the present study lies in the following aspects.

Firstly, this research adopted a new vocabulary assessing instrument, the VKS test, to measure the depth of word knowledge. The vocabulary tests used in previous studies are confined to L1 equivalents translation or multiple-choice items which can only assess the meaning or form of a word. However, according to Nation's (1990) categorization, word knowledge is a multidimensional concept. Knowing a word does not only mean knowing its meaning and form, but also entails acquiring its syntactical and functional aspects of knowledge. Therefore, instruments used in previous studies fail to present a comprehensive report of whether learners have gained a word's multiple aspects of knowledge. In contrast, the VKS test used in this study can assess multiple facets (form, meaning, position/syntax, and function) of the word knowledge. Five categories used in this test can also reveal the detailed information of word knowledge development in both receptive and productive aspects. Categories 1 and 3 relate primarily to the receptive aspect of word knowledge. Categories 4 and 5 assess the productive aspect of word knowledge. In the present study, it is found that different learning conditions may have the same impact on acquisition of receptive knowledge of a word in the semantic aspect, but they show different impacts on acquisition of productive knowledge of a word in grammatical or functional aspects.

Secondly, two supplemental word tests, the dictation test and collocation matching test, were adopted in the present study to attain more detailed information of learners' formal and syntactical aspects of word knowledge. Since the VKS test could only assess the receptive knowledge of orthography, a dictation test was used in this research to assess the productive knowledge of orthography. A collocation matching test was also adopted in this research to assess learners' receptive knowledge of syntax.

Thirdly, computer software and an online corpus were used in this study. "Vocabprofile" (Cobb, 2007) was used to check out the frequency of target words in the text. This software has been widely used by overseas SLA researchers but received little attention in the SLA research community in China. The online COCA was also used in this study to provide learners with more sufficient and authentic instances in the L2 vocabulary learning process.

6.4 Pedagogical implications

This research proposes some pedagogical implications for L2 vocabulary acquisition in specific learning context in China. The implications can be formulated as follows:

Firstly, both the input and output processing tasks are of vital importance for enhancing deep elaboration of the vocabulary knowledge.

On the one hand, sufficient input processing is necessary for learners to formulate their hypotheses on the target words. On the other hand, the output tasks provide learners with opportunities to test their hypotheses on the target word knowledge. Moreover, the feedback on the output from their instructors or peers may deepen or enrich their understanding of the target word knowledge. The joint impact of input and output processing tasks may enhance the input-to-intake transition process and be beneficial for long-term storage of the target word knowledge.

Secondly, sentence-level instances are more effective and efficient for word knowledge encoding in L2 vocabulary learning context, especially in the classroom settings. Corpus is an optimal choice for instances collection, in which numerous authentic sentence-level instances can be searched out by typing in a target word as a keyword. Learners or instructors can also find the most frequent collocates of the target word by using specific concordance functions in the corpus. The abundant examples provide learners with comprehensive information of multiple facets of target word knowledge, such as a word's different meanings in various contexts, its grammatical patterns, collocations or appropriateness of use in distinctive registers.

Thirdly, it is suggested that instructors can adopt the inductive learning method in the L2 vocabulary learning context. The findings in the present study imply that the inductive cognitive mode is more beneficial for acquisition and retention of L2 vocabulary knowledge. In contrast with the rule-based teaching method which advocates explicit rules presentation, the inductive learning context is more learner-centered. It encourages learners to extract word knowledge from the instances and construct their own concepts or understanding of a target word. Thus, learners' learning motivation and interest can be greatly enhanced. More attention and cognitive load are involved in the inductive learning, which can greatly deepen the elaboration of the target words and facilitate the input-to-intake transition process.

Fourthly, compared with the traditional word list, the word journal paper is a better type of layout for new word presentation. In the traditional word list, multiple facets of word knowledge (such as the written forms, pronunciation, meaning, grammatical categories and example sentences) are directly presented to learners. This type of layout is concordant with the explicit rule-based teaching method, which has been proved to be ineffective on L2 vocabulary learning and retention in the present study. In contrast, the word journal paper is concordant with the inductive learning method. In the word journal paper, only the words with their pronunciation and example sentences are provided. Blanks and brackets are designed, in which the meaning, collocation and other aspects of word knowledge are required to be written by learners during the learning process.

Finally, it is suggested that instructors or teachers should change their role from dominators of the class into learners' assistants in the L2 vocabulary learning process. Instead of cramming learners with rules or word knowledge, teachers should encourage learners to extract word knowledge from instances by themselves. Teachers are responsible for providing feedback to learners' hypotheses on the target word knowledge and providing other related knowledge which is necessary but does not appear in the example sentences. It is also very important for teachers to draw learners' attention to some aspects of word knowledge which are often ignored by learners.

6.5 Limitations of the book

Even though great efforts have been made to avoid any deficiency, the present study still confronts some inevitable limitations which are listed as follows.

The one-week's interval between the pre-test and the immediate post-test was not long enough to eliminate the possibility that learners might remember the target words used in the pre-test. The sense of frustration for failing to provide the meaning of most words in the pre-test might prompt some learners to pay special attention to the target words or even consult the dictionary for the words' meaning.

Although the reliability and validity assessment of vocabulary knowledge have been widely acknowledged by many researchers, the VKS test still has some limitations in assessing depth of word knowledge. On the one hand, the self-report mode of the VKS test may inevitably lead to some subjectiveness in the data, especially for the answers in Categories 1 and 2. Learners may think that they have seen or known a target word which is actually new to them, due to the similar form of the words. On the other hand, it seems to be difficult to obtain detailed information of some aspects of word knowledge such as the grammatical and syntactical aspects of knowledge. Different types of errors, such as incorrect use of grammatical forms or collocates, are all categorized on the same scale. This type of scoring method mixes the different types of errors together and inhibits the in-depth analysis of learners' performance in each facets of word knowledge.

Although attention has been proved to be a critical factor in L2 vocabulary learning, no questionnaires, retrospective reports or other instruments were used in this research to specify different degrees of attention allocated to different aspects of word knowledge. Only an informal interview which involved some questions on learners' attention to distinctive aspects of word knowledge was conducted after the treatments.

Despite the effectiveness of reconstruction tasks on promoting the use of target words, there seemed to be some potential risks that this type of output task might confine learners' production to limited types of sentence structures or registers. Other possible syntactical patterns or collocations which learners could use based on their own hypotheses on the target words could not be revealed in the reconstruction tasks.

In Experiment 2, only the VKS instrument was used to assess learners' depth of vocabulary knowledge acquisition after the treatment. Since the treatment conducted in the comprehensive group consisted of both input processing and reconstruction tasks, it costed more time to complete the treatment than in Experiment 1. During the settled lecture time, there was no more time left for learners to finish the other supplementary tests that had been used in Experiment 1.

It could be better if more target words were used in this study. Only 12 target words were chosen in this research, considering that it might take too much time for learners to encode so many words elaborately. As to the number of words acquired, the differences between the experimental groups in Experiment 2 were not so obvious, although they reached the significant level.

6.6 Recommendations for further research

This research has drawn some conclusions in the L2 vocabulary acquisition within the information processing framework and indicates some directions for further studies on L2 vocabulary acquisition from a cognitive perspective. As was mentioned in the previous section, some limitations need to be removed in further studies. In addition, some recommendations for further research will be discussed in this section.

Due to the fact that the VKS test is far from enough to assess all aspects of word knowledge, it seems to be necessary to adopt more varied test instruments in further studies to achieve more comprehensive assessment of depth of word knowledge. The receptive and productive knowledge of a word in different aspects is also expected to be assessed. However, the design of such a battery of tests seems to be a tough job. Webb (2006) has designed a series of subtests to assess three levels of word knowledge (form, position, and meaning) from both receptive and productive aspects according to Nation's (1990) dimensional-based word knowledge categorization. The problem is that both design and administration of so many vocabulary subtests are quite time-consuming. It is difficult to assure the reliability and validity of each subtest. Further studies are needed to be made on the design of vocabulary assessing instrument which could be more effective and efficient.

A second focus for further study might be quantifying the role of attention on different aspects of word knowledge by using questionnaires, retrospective reports, or any other instruments. Qualitative studies on the roles of attention in grammatical learning have been conducted by many researchers (Izumi, 2003; Song, 2006). There are few similar studies done in the L2 vocabulary acquisition field, although attention is also regarded as a critical factor affecting vocabulary learning. More factors could also be contributed to the design of feasible questionnaires which can effectively explore roles of attention in acquisition of specific aspects of word knowledge.

In addition, the participants in this research were freshmen in college with intermediate English proficiency level. Therefore, similar research might be conducted in high school or elementary school to testify whether the learning method recommended in this research is effective for learners with different English proficiency levels.

Bibliography

Aitchison, J. (1987). *Words in the Mind: An Introduction to the Mental Lexicon*. Oxford: Basil Blackwell.

Alanen, R. (1995). Input enhancement and rule presentation in second language acquisition. In R. Schmidt (Ed.), *Attention and Awareness in Foreign Language Learning* (pp. 259-299). Honolulu, HI: University of Hawai'i Press.

Anderson, J. R. (1983). A spreading activation theory of memory. *Journal of Verbal Learning and Verbal Behavior,* 22, 261-295.

Anderson, R. C., Freebody, P. (1981).Vocabulary knowledge. In J. Guthrie (Ed.), *Comprehension and Teaching: Research Reviews* (pp.77-117). Newark, DE: International Reading Association.

Bai, L. (2002). *The Roles of Breadth and Depth of Vocabulary Knowledge in Reading Comprehension*. Unpublished M.A thesis, Northwest Normal University, Lanzhou.

Bai, R. L. (2005). Word association in foreign language vocabulary acquisition. *Foreign Languages and Their Teaching*, 1, 28-31. [白人立，2005. 词汇联想反应 . 外语与外语教学（1）：28-31.]

Barcroft, J. (1999). Processing resources and L2 lexical acquisition in three writing tasks. Paper presented at the Second Language Research Forum, Minneapolis, MN.

Barcroft, J. (2000). The generation effect in L2 lexical acquisition. Paper presented at the Second Language Research Forum, Madison, WI.

Barcroft, J. (2002). Semantic and structural elaboration in L2 lexical acquisition. *Language Learning* ,52(2), 323-363.

Barcroft, J. (2004). Effects of sentence making in second language lexical acquisition. *Second Language Research,* 20(49), 303-334.

Bruner, J. (1983). *Child's Talk: Learning to Use Language*. New York: W. W. Norton & Company.

Carton, A. (1971). Inferencing: a process in using and learning language. In P. Pimsleer & T. Ouinn. (Eds.), *The Psychology Second Language Learning* (pp.45-58). Cambridge: Cambridge University Press.

Chapelle, C. A. (1994). Are C-tests valid measures for L2 vocabulary research? *Second Language Research,* 10, 157-187.

Chapelle, C. A. (1998). Construct definition and validity inquiry in SLA research. In L. F. Bachman & A. D. Cohen (Eds.), *Second Language Acquisition and Language Testing Interfaces* (pp. 32-70). Cambridge: Cambridge University Press.

Cheng, S. W. (2003). Application of the output hypothesis theory to listening teaching. *Journal of Anhui University*, 3, 75-78. [程少武，2003. 语言输出理论在听力教学中的应用研究 . 安徽大学学报（哲学社会科学版）(3): 75-78.]

Clark, E. V. (1993). *The Lexicon in Acquisition*. Cambridge: Cambridge University Press.

Cobb, T. (2007). The Complete Lexical Tutor. Retrieved from http://www.lextutor.ca/.

Cohen, A. D. (1987). The use of verbal and imagery mnemonics in second language vocabulary learning. *Studies in Second Language Acquisition,* 9(1), 43-62.

Cohen, A. D. (1998). *Strategies in Learning and Using a Second Language*. London: Longman.

Coomber, J. E., Ramstad, D. A., & Sheets, D. R. (1986). Elaboration in vocabulary learning: a comparison of three rehearsal methods. *Research in the Teaching of English,* 20, 281-293.

Corson, D. (1997). The learning and use of academic English words. *Language Learning,* 47(4), 671-718.

Craik, F. I. M., & Lockhart, R. S. (1972). Levels of processing: A framework for memory research. *Journal of Verbal Learning and Verbal Behavior,* 11(671-684).

Craik, F. I. M. (1979). Levels of processing: overview and closing comments. In L. S. Cermak & F. I. M. Craik (Eds.), *Levels of Processing in Human Memory* (pp. 447-461). Hillsdale, NJ: Lawrence Erlbaum Associates Inc.

Craik, F. I. M., & Lockhart, R. S. (2002). Levels of processing: Past, present ... and future?. *Memory*, 10, 305-318.

Craik, F. I. M., & Lockhart, R. S. (1975). Depth of processing and the retention of words in episodic memory. *Journal of Experimental Psychology (General),* 104(3), 268-294.

Cronbach, L. J. (1942). An analysis of techniques for diagnostic vocabulary testing. *Journal of Educational Research*, 36(3), 206-217.

Cui, Y. Y. (2008). An exploration into the development of lexical competence of Chinese tertiary English majors. Qingdao: China Ocean University Press. [崔艳嫣, 2008. 中国英语专业学生词汇能力发展研究 . 青岛：中国海洋大学出版社 .]

de Bot, K. (1996). The psycholinguistics of the output hypothesis. *Language Learning*, 46(3), 529-555.

de Bot, K., Paribakht, T., & Wesche, M. (1997). Toward a lexical processing model for the study of second language vocabulary acquisition: Evidence from ESL reading. *Studies in Second Language Acquisition,* 19, 309-329.

de la Fuente, M. J. (2006). Classroom L2 vocabulary acquisition: investigating the role of pedagogical tasks and form-focused instruction.

Language Teaching Research, 10(3), 263-295.

DeKeyser, R. M., & Sokalski, K. J. (1996). The differential role of comprehension and production practice. *Language Learning,* 46(4), 613-642.

Doughty, C. (1991). Second language instruction does make a difference. *Studies in Second Language Acquisition,* 13, 431-469.

Doughty, C. (2001). Cognitive underpinnings of focus on form. In P. Robinson (Ed.), *Cognition and Second Language Instruction* (pp. 206-238). Cambridge, UK: Cambridge University Press.

Doughty, C. (2004). Effects of instruction on learning a second language: a critique of instructed SLA research. In B. J. Williams, S. Rott & M. Overstreet (Eds.), *Form-Meaning Connections in Second Language Acquisition* (pp. 181-202). Mahwah, NJ: Lawrence Erlbaum Associate.

Doughty, C., & Williams, J. (1998). *Focus on Form in Second Language Acquisition*. Cambridge, UK: Cambridge University Press.

Doughty, C., & Williams, J. (1998). Pedagogical choices in focus on form. In C. Doughty. & J. Williams (Eds.), *Focus on Form in Classroom Second Language Acquisition* (pp. 197-261). New York: Cambridge University Press.

Dupuy, B., & Krashen, S. (1993). Incidental vocabulary acquisition in French as a foreign language. *Applied Language Learning,* 4, 55-63.

Ellis, N. C. (1994). *Implicit and Explicit Learning of Languages*. San Diego, CA: Academic Press.

Ellis, R. (2005). Principles of instructed language learning. *System*, 2(33), 209-224.

Ellis, R., & He, X. (1999). The role of modified input and output in the incidental acquisition of word meanings. *Studies in Second Language Acquisition,* 21, 285-301.

Eysenck. (1982). Incidental learning and orienting tasks. In C. R. Puff (Ed.),

Handbook of Research Methods in Human Memory and Cognition (pp. 197-228). New York: Academic Press.

Eysenck, M. W. (1978). Levels of processing: a critique. *British Journal of Psychology*, 69, 157-169.

Faerch, K., Haastrup, K., & Phillipson, R. (1984). *Learner Language and Language Learning*. Copenhagen: Multilingual Matters.

Fang, L. L. (2004). The length-approach writing instruction in college English classes. *Foreign Language World*, 3, 40-45. [方 玲 玲, 2004. "写长法"在大学英语教学中的应用研究. 外语界 (3): 40-45.]

Feng, J. Y. & Huang, J. (2004). The effect of output tasks on acquisition of linguistic forms. *Modern Foreign Languages*, 2, 196-220. [冯纪元, 黄娇, 2004. 语言输出活动对语言形式习得的影响. 现代外语 (2): 196-220.]

Fotos, S., & Ellis, R. (1991). Communicating about grammar: a task-based approach. *TESOL Quarterly,* 25, 605-628.

Fox, J (1984). Computer-assisted vocabulary learning. *English Language Journal,* 31(1), 27-33.

Fraser, C. A. (1999). Lexical processing strategy use and vocabulary learning through reading. *Studies in Second Language Acquisition,* 21, 225-241.

Gass, S. (1997). *Input, Interation, and the Second Language Learner*. Hillsdale, NJ: Erlbaum.

Gass, S. (1999). Discussion: incidental vocabulary learning. *Studies in Second Language Acquisition,* 21, 319-333.

Gass, S., Carolyn, M., Dennis, P., & Larry, S. (1988). *Variation in Second Language Acquisition: Psycholinguistic Issues*. Clevedon: Multilingual Matters.

Gass, S., & Madden, C. (1985). *Input in Second Language Acquisition*. Rowley: Newbury House.

Gass, S., Sorace, A., & Selinker, L. (1999). *Second Language Learning: Data Analysis* (2nd ed.). Mahwah, NJ: Erlbaum.

Gass, S. M., & Selinker, L. (1994). *Second Language Acquisition: An Introductory Course*. Amsterdam: John Benjamins.

Gass, S. M., & Selinker, L. (2001). *Second Language Acquisition: An Introductory Course.*(2nd ed.). Mahwah, NJ: Erlbaum.

Goldinger, S. D. (1998). Echoes of echoes? An episodic theory of lexical access. *Psychological Review,* 105(2), 251-279.

Goulden, R., Nation, P., & Read, J. (1990). How large can a receptive vocabulary be?. *Applied Linguistics,* 11(4), 341-363.

Greidanus, T., & Nienhuis, L. (2001). Testing the quality of word knowledge in a second language by means of word associations: types of distractors and types of associations. *The Modern Language Journal,* 85, 567-577.

Gu, Y., & Johnson, R. K. (1996). Vocabulary learning strategies and language learning outcomes. *Language Learning* 46, 643-679.

Haastrup, K. (1991). *Lexical Inferencing Procedures or Talking about Words.* Tübingen: Gunter Narr.

Haastrup, K., & Henriksen, B. (2000). Vocabulary acquisition: acquiring depth of knowledge through network building. *International Journal of Applied Linguistics,* 10, 221-240.

Hancin-Bhatt, B., & Nagy, W. (1994). Lexical transfer and second-language morphological development. *Applied Psycholinguistics,* 15, 289-310.

Harrington, M., & Dennis, S. (2002). Input-driven language learning. *Studies in Second Language Acquisition,* 24, 261-268.

Hazenberg, S., & Hulstijn, J. H. (1996). Defining a minimal receptive second-language vocabulary for non-native university students: an empirical investigation. *Applied Linguistics,* 17(2), 145-163.

Henriksen, B. (1999). Three dimensions of vocabulary development. *Studies in Second Language Acquisition,* 21(2), 303-317.

Huckin, T., & Bloch, J. (1993). Strategies for inferring word meaning in context: a cognitive model. In T. Huckin, M. Haynes & J. Coady (Eds.), *Second Language Reading and Vocabulary Learning* (pp. 153-180). Norwood, NJ: Ablex Publishing.

Huckin, T., & Coady, J. (1999). Incidental vocabulary acquisition in a second language: a review. *Studies in Second Language Acquisition,* 21, 181-193.

Hulme, C., Maughan, S., & Brown, G. D. A. (1991). Memory for familiar and unfamiliar words: evidence for a long-term memory contribution to short-term memory span. *Journal of Memory and Language,* 30, 685-701.

Hulstijn, J. (2001). Intention and incidental second language vocabulary learning: a reappraisal of elaboration, rehearsal, and automaticity. In P. Robinson (Ed.), *Cognition and Second Language Instruction* (pp. 258-286). Cambridge: Cambridge University Press.

Hulstijn, J. H. (1992). Retention of inferred and given word meanings: experiments in incidental vocabulary learning. In P. J. L. Arnaud & H. Bejoint (Eds.), *Vocabulary and Applied Linguistics* (pp. 113-125). London: Macmillan.

Hulstijn, J. H., & Trompetter, P. (1998). Incidental learning of second language vocabulary in computer-assisted reading and writing tasks. In D. Albrechtsen, B. Henriksen, I.M. Mees & E. Poulsen (Eds.), *Perspectives on Foreign and Second Language Pedagogy* (pp. 191-200). Odense: Odense University Press.

Izumi, S. (2002). Output, input enhancement, and the noticing hypothesis: an experimental study on ESL relativization. *Studies in Second Language Acquisition,* 24, 541-577.

Izumi, S. (2003). Comprehension and production processes in second language learning: in search of the psycholinguistic rationale of the output hypothesis. *Applied Linguistics,* 24(2), 168-196.

Izumi, S., & Bigelow, M. (2000). Does output promote noticing and second language acquisition. *TESOL Quarterly,* 2(34), 239-273.

Jenkins, J., M. Stein, & K.Wysocki. (1984). Learning vocabulary through reading. *American Educational Research Journal,* 21(4), 767-787.

Johnson, M. (2004). *A Philosophy of Second Language Acquisition.* New Haven: Yale University Press.

Kaya, T. (2006). *The Effectiveness of Adaptive Computer Use for Learning Vocabulary.* Northern Arizona University, Flagstaff.

Krashen, S. (1982). *Principles and Practice in Second Language Acquisition.* New York: Pergamon.

Krashen, S. (1984). *Writing: Research, Theory and Applications.* Laredo: Beverly Hills.

Krashen, S. (1985). *The Input Hypothesis: Issues and Implications.* London: Longman.

Krashen, S. (1989). We acquire vocabulary and spelling by reading: additional evidence for the input hypothesis. *The Modern Language Journal,* 73, 440-464.

Krashen, S. D. (1998). Comprehensible output. *System*, 2(26), 175-182.

Kwon, S. H. (2006). *Roles of Output and Task Design on Second Language Vocabulary Acquisition.* Gainesville: University of Florida.

Laufer, B. (1989). What percentage of text-lexis is essential for comprehension?. In C. Lauren & M. Nordman (Eds.), *Special Language: From Humans Thinking to Thinking Machines* (pp.316-323). Clevedon: Multilingual Matters.

Laufer, B. (1991). The development of L2 lexis in the expression of the advanced learner. *The Modern Language Journal,* 75(4), 440-448.

Laufer, B. (1992). How much lexis is necessary for reading comprehension. In H. Bejoint & P. Arnaud (Eds.), *Vocabulary and Applied Linguistics* (pp. 126-132). London: MacMillan.

Laufer, B. (1997). The lexical plight in second language reading: words you don't know, and words you can't guess. In J. Coady & T. Huckin (Eds.), *Second Language Vocabulary Acquisition: A Rationale for Pedagogy* (pp. 20-34). New York: Cambridge Press.

Laufer, B. (1998). The relationship between passive and active vocabularies: effects of language learning context. *Language Learning,* 48(3), 365-391.

Laufer, B. (2003). Vocabulary acquisition in a second language: do learners really acquire most vocabulary by reading? Some empirical evidence. *The Canadian Modern Language Review,* 59(4), 567-587.

Laufer, B., Elder, C., Hill, K., & Congdon, P. (2004). Size and strength: do we need both to measure vocabulary knowledge? *Language Testing,* 21(2), 202-226.

Laufer, B., & Hulstijn, J. (2001). Incidental vocabulary acquisition in a second language: the construct of task-induced involvement. *Applied Linguistics,* 22, 1-26.

Laufer, B., & Paribakht., T. S. (1998). Relationship between passive and active vocabularies: effects of language learning context. *Language Learning,* 48, 365-391.

Leow, R. (1997). The effects of input enhancement and text length on adult L2 readers' comprehension and intake in second language acquisition. *Applied Language Learning,* 8, 151-182.

Leow, R. (2001). Do learners notice enhanced forms while interacting with the L2?: an online and offline study of the role of written input enhancement in L2 reading. *Hispania*, 84, 496-509.

Leow, R., Egi, T., Nuevo, A., & Tsai, Y. (2003). The roles of textual enhancement and type of linguistic item in adult L2 learners' comprehension and intake. *Applied Language Learning,* 13(2), 1-16.

Levelt, W. (1989). *Speaking: From Intention to Articulation*. Cambridge, MA: The MIT Press.

Levelt, W. (1993). Language use in normal speakers and its disorders. In G. Blanken, J. Dittman, H. Grimm, J. Marshall & C. Wallesch (Eds.), *Linguistic Disorders and Pathologies: An International Handbook* (pp.1-15). Berlin: de Gruyter Mouton.

Levelt, W., Roelofs, A., & Meyer, A. (1999). A theory of lexical access in speech production. *Bebavioral and Brain Sciences,* 22, 1-75.

Levine, A., & Reves, T. (1990). Does the method of vocabulary presentation make a difference? *TESL Canada Journal,* 8(1), 37-51.

Li, H. (2002). The cognitive basis of comprehensible output hypothesis. *Foreign Languages and Their Teaching*, 2, 10-16. [李红，2002. 可理解输出假设的认知基础 . 外语与外语教学（2）：10-16.]

Li, Z-Y. (2004). Assessing the roles of breadth and depth of vocabulary knowledge in writing in second language acquisition. Unpublished M.A. thesis, Yangzhou University, Yangzhou.

Liu, C. (2008). *Test Source for IELTS. Beijing:* Science Press. [刘创，2008. 雅思阅读真题题源 . 北京：科学出版社 .]

Liu, C-Y. (2006). Researching language output as an active part in SLA: a task-based approach. unpublished thesis. Shanghai International Studies University, Shanghai.

Lockhart, R. S., Craik, F. I. M., & Jacoby, L. L. (1975). Depth of processing in recognition and recall: some aspects of a general memory system. In J. Brown (Ed.), *Recognition and Recall* (pp.75-102). London: Wiley.

Long, M. (1991). Focus on form: a design feature in language teaching methodology. In K. de Bot, D. Coste, C. Kramsch & R. Ginsberg (Eds.), *Foreign Language Research in a Crosscultural Perspective* (pp. 39-52). Amsterdam: John Benjamins.

Long, M., & Robinson, P. (1998). Focus on form: theory, research and practice. In C. Doughty & J. Williams (Eds.), *Focus on Form in Classroom Second Language Acquisition* (pp. 85-113). Cambridge, UK: Cambridge University Press.

Loschky, D., & Bley-Vroman., R. (1993). Grammar and task-based methodology. In G. Crookes & S. M. Gass (Eds.), *Tasks in a Pedagogical Context* (pp.123-163). Bristol: Multilingual Matters.

Mackey, A. (1999). Input, interaction and second language development: an empirical study of question formation in ESL. *Studies in Second Language Acquisition,* 21(4), 557-581.

Mackey, A., & Gass, S. (2005). *Second Language Research: Methodology and Design*. Mahwah, NJ: Lawrence Erlbaum Associates.

MacWhinney, B. (1997). Second language acqusition and the competition model. In A. M. B. de Groot & J. F. Kroll (Eds.), *Tutorials in Bilingualism: Psycholinguistic Perspectives* (pp.113-142). Mahwah, NJ: Lawrence Erlbaum Associates.

Mathews, R. C., Buss, R. R., Stanley, W. B., Blanchard-Fields, F., Cho, J. R., & Druhan, B. (1989). Role of implicit and explicit processes in learning from examples: a synergistic effect. *Journal of Experimental Psychology: Learning, Memory, & Cognition,* 15(6), 1083-1100.

McCarthy, M. J. (1990). *Vocabulary*. Oxford: Oxford University Press.

McGeoch, J. A. (1942). *The Psychology of Human Learning: An Introduction*. New York: Longmans Green.

McKeown, M. G., Beck, I. L., Omanson, R. G., & Pople, M. T. (1985). Some effects of the nature and frequency of vocabulary instruction on the knowledge and use of words. *Reading Research Quarterly,* 20(5), 522-535.

McLaughlin, B. (1990). Restructuring. *Applied Linguistics,* 11, 113-128.

Meara, P. (1984). Review of teaching vocabulary by M. J. Wallace. *System,* 12(1), 185-186.

Meara, P. (1996). The dimensions of lexical competence. In G. Brown, K. Malmkjaer & J. Williams (Eds.), *Performance and Competence in Second Language Acquisition* (pp. 35-53). Cambridge: Cambridge University Press.

Meara, P., Lightbown, P., & Halter, R. H. (1997). Classrooms as lexical environments. *Language Teaching Research,* 1(1), 28-47.

Melka, F. (1997). Receptive vs. productive aspects of vocabulary. In N. Schmitt & M. McCarthy (Eds.), *Vocabulary: Description, Acquisition, and Pedagogy* (pp. 84-102). New York: Cambridge University Press.

Nagy, W. E., & Anderson, R. C. (1984). How many words are there in printed school English? *Reading Research Quarterly,* 19, 304-330.

Nagy, W. E., & Herman, P. A. (1987). Breadth and depth of vocabulary knowledge: implications for acquisition and instruction. In M. McKeown & M. Curtis (Eds.), *The Nature of Vocabulary Acquisition* (pp. 19-35). Hillsdale, NJ: Erlbaum Associates.

Nagy, W. E., Herman, P. A., & Anderson, R. C. (1985). Learning words from context. *Reading Research Quarterly,* 20, 233-253.

Nation, I. S. P. (1990). *Teaching and Learning Vocabulary*. New York: Heinle & Heinle.

Nation, I. S. P. (2001). *Learning Vocabulary in Another Language*. Cambridge: Cambridge University Press.

Nation, P., & Wang, Ming-Tzu, K. (1999). Graded readers and vocabulary. *Reading in a Foreign Language,* 12, 355-379.

Nobuyoshi, J., & Ellis, R. (1993). Focused communication tasks and second language acquisition. *ELT Journal,* 47(3), 203-210.

Overstreet, M. (1998). Text enhancement and content familiarity: the focus of learner attention. *Spanish Applied Linguistics,* 2, 229-258.

Palmberg, R. (1987). Patterns of vocabulary development in foreign-language learners. *Studies in Second Language Acquisition,* 9, 201-220.

Paribakht, T. S., & Wesche, M. (1993). Reading comprehension and second language development in a comprehension-based ESL programme. *TESL Canada Journal,* 11, 9-27.

Paribakht, T. S., & Wesche, M. (1997). Vocabulary enhancement activities and reading for meaning in second language vocabulary acquisition. In J. Coady & T. Huckin (Eds.), *Second Language Vocabulary Acquisition: A Rationale for Pedagogy* (pp. 174-202). New York: Cambridge University Press.

Paribakht, T. S., & Wesche, M. (1999). Reading and "incidental" L2 vocabulary acquisition: an introspective study of lexical inferencing. *Studies in Second Language Acquisition,* 21(2), 195-224.

Parry, K. (1997). Vocabulary and comprehension: two portraits. In J. Coady & T. Huckin (Eds.), *Second Language Vocabulary Acquisition.*(pp.55-68). New York: Cambridge University Press.

Piaget, J. (1972). Intellectual evolution from adolescence to adulthood. *Human Development,* 15(1), 1-12.

Pica, T. (1994). Research on negotiation: what does it reveal about second-language learning conditions, processes, and outcomes? *Language Learning,* 44(3), 493-527.

Pica, T., Holliday, L., Lewis, N., & Morgenthaler, L. (1989). Comprehensible output as an outcome of linguistic demands on the learner. *Studies in Second Language Acquisition,* 11, 63-90.

Pornpibul, N. (2002). The role of writing in EFL students' learning from texts: a case study in a Thai university. *Research Abstracts International,* 63(12), 4195A.

Prince, P. (1996). Second language vocabulary learning: the role of context versus translations as a function of proficiency. *The Modern Language Journal,* 80, 478-493.

Qian, D. D. (1999). Assessing the roles of depth and breadth of vocabulary knowledge in reading comprehension. *Canadian Modern Language Review,* 56, 282-308.

Qian, D. D. (2002). Investigating the relationship between vocabulary knowledge and academic reading performance: an assessment perspective. *Language Learning,* 52, 513-536.

Qian, D. D., & Schedl, M. (2004). Evaluation of an in-depth vocabulary knowledge measure for assessing reading performance. *Language Testing,* 21(1), 28-52.

Read, J. (2000). *Assessing Vocabulary.* Cambridge: Cambridge University Press.

Read, J. (2004). Plumbing the depths: how should the construct of vocabulary knowledge be defined?. In P. Bogaards & B. Laufer (Eds.), *Vocabulary in a Second Language: Selection, Acquisition and Testing* (pp. 209-227). Amsterdam: John Benjamins.

Read, J., & Chapelle, C. A. (2001). A framework for second language vocabulary assessment. *Language Testing,* 18, 1-32.

Reber, A. S. (1989). Implicit learning and tacit knowledge. *Journal of Experimental Psychology (General),* 118(3), 219-235.

Richards, J. C. (1976). The role of vocabulary teaching. *TESOL Quarterly,* 10(1), 77-89.

Robinson, P. (1996). Learning simple and complex second language rules under implicit, incidental, rule-search, and instructed conditions. *Studies in Second Language Acquisition,* 18, 27-67.

Robinson, P. (2001). *Cognition and Second Language Instruction.* Cambridge: Cambridge University Press.

Robinson, P. (2003). Attention and memory during SLA. In C. D. M. Long (Ed.), *The Handbook of SLA* (pp. 630-678). Oxford, UK: Blackwell Publishers.

Robinson, P., & Ha, M. (1993). *Cognitive Load and the Route-Marked Not-*

marked Map Task. Unpublished work, University of Hawaii at Manoa, Honolulu.

Rosa, E., & Neill, M. D. O. (1999). Explicitness, intake and the issue of awareness: another piece to the puzzle. *Studies in Second Language Acquisition,* 21, 511-556.

Rott, S. (2004). A comparison of output interventions and un-enhanced reading conditions on vocabulary acquisition and text comprehension. *The Canadian Modern Language Review,* 61(2), 169-202.

Saragi, T., Nation, I. S. P., & Meister, G. F. (1978). Vocabulary learning and reading. *System,* 6(2), 72-78.

Schmidt. (1990). The Role of consciousness in second language learning. *Applied Linguistics,* 11, 129-158.

Schmidt, R. (1993). Awareness and second language acquisition. *Annual Review of Applied Linguistics,* 13, 206-226.

Schmidt, R. (1994). Deconstructing consciousness in search of useful definitions for applied linguistics. *AILA Review,* 11, 11-26.

Schmidt, R. (2001). Attention. In P. Robinson (Ed.), *Cognition and Second Language Instruction* (pp. 3-32). Cambridge, UK: Cambridge University Press.

Schmidt, R. W. (1995). Consciousness and foreign language learning: a tutorial on the role of attention and awareness in learning. In R. Schmidt (Ed.), *Attention and Awareness in Foreign Language Learning* (pp. 1-63). Honolulu, Hawaii: University of Hawaii, Second Language Teaching & Curriculum Centre.

Schmitt, N. (1998). Quantifying word association responses: what is native-like? *System,* 26: 389-401.

Schmitt, N. (2000). *Vocabulary in Language Teaching.* Cambridge: Cambridge University Press.

Schmitt, N., & McCarthy, M. (1997). *Vocabulary: Description, Acquisition and Pedagogy*. Cambridge: Cambridge University Press.

Schmitt, N., Schmitt, D., & Clapham, C. (2001). Developing and exploring the behavior of two new versions of the Vocabulary Levels Test. *Language Testing,* 18, 55-88.

Schouten-van Parreren, C. (1996). Vocabulary Learning and Metacognition. In K. Sajavaara & C. Fairweather (Eds.), *Approaches to Second Language Acquisition* (pp. 63-39). Finland: University of Jyvaskyla.

Schwartz, B. D. (1993). On explicit and negative data effecting and affecting competence and linguistic behavior. *Studies in Second Language Acquisition,* 15, 147-163.

Scott, J. A., & Nagy, W. E. (1994). Vocabulary development. In A. C. Purves, Papa, L., & Jordan, S. (Eds.), *Encyclopedia of English Studies and Language Arts* (Vol. 2, pp. 1242-1244). New York: Scholastic.

Scovel, T. (1998). *Psycholinguistics*. Oxford: Oxford University Press.

Segalowitz, N., Watson, V., & Segalowitz, S. (1995). Vocabulary skill: single-case assessment of automaticity of word recognition in a timed lexical decision task. *Second Language Research,* 11(2), 121-136.

Shehadeh, A. (1999). Non-native-speakers' production of modified comprehensible output and second language learning. *Language Learning,* 49(4), 627-675.

Shook, D. (1994). FL/L2 reading, grammatical information, and the input-to-intake phenomenon. *Applied Language Learning,* 10, 39-76.

Shu, W. M. (2006). *Incidental Vocabulary Acquisition through Reading: Effects of Exposure Frequency and Contextual Richness*. unpublished thesis. Guangdong University of Foreign Studies, Guangzhou.

Sinclair, J. (1991). *Corpus Concordance Collocation*. Oxford: Corpus Concordance Collocation.

Skehan, P. (1998). *A Cognitive Approach to Language Learning.* Oxford: Oxford University Press.

Slobin, D. I. (1973). Cognitive prerequisites for the development of grammar. In C. A. Ferguson & D. I. Slobin (Eds.), *Studies of Child Language Development* (pp.175-208). New York: Holt, Rinehart & Winston.

Snellings, P., Gelderenet, A. V., & Glopper., K. D. (2004). Validating a test of second language written lexical retrieval: a new measure of fluency in written language production. *Language Testing,* 21(2), 174-201.

Song, X. P. (2008). *Input Enhancement, Output and Noticing*. Unpublished Ph. D. research, Shanghai International Studies University, Shanghai.

Sun, J. (2006). An experimental study of corpus concordance of English vocabulary teaching in high school. Retrieved from http://acad.cnki.net/kns55/detail/detail.aspx?dbcode=CMFD&QueryID=23&CurRe c=1.

Sutherland, N. S. (1972). Object recognition. In E. C. C. M. P. Friedman (Ed.), *Handbook of Perception* (Vol. 3, pp.157-185). New York: Academic Press.

Swain, M. (1985). Communicative competence: some roles of comprehensible input and comprehensible output in its development. In S. Gass & C. Madden (Eds.), *Input in Second Language Acquisition* (pp.35-70). Rowley, MA: Newbury House.

Swain, M. (1995). Three functions of output in second language learning. In G. C. B. Seidlhofer (Ed.), *Principles and Practice in the Study of Language* (pp.125-144). Oxford: Oxford University Press.

Swain, M. (1998). Focus on form through conscious reflection. In C. Doughty & J. Williams (Eds.), *Focus on Form in Classroom Second Language Acquisition* (pp. 64-81). Cambridge: Cambridge University Press.

Swain, M. (2000). The output hypothesis and beyond: mediating acquisition through collaborative dialogue. In J. P. Lantolf (Ed.), *Sociocultural Theory and Second Language Learning* (pp. 97-114). Oxford: Oxford University Press.

Swain, M. (2005). Verbal protocols: what does it mean for research to use speaking as a data collection tool. In M. Chaloub-Deville, M. Chapelle & P. Duff (Eds.), *Inference and Generalizability In Applied Linguistics: Multiple Research Perspectives* (pp. 97-113). Amsterdam: Benjamins.

Swain, M., & Lapkin, S. (1986). Immersion French at the secondary level: 'the goods' and 'the bads'. *Contact,* 5(3), 2-9.

Swain, M., & Lapkin, S. (1995). Problems in output and the cognitive processes they generate: a step towards second language learning. *Applied Linguistics,* 16(3), 371-391.

Tarone., E. (1985). Variability in interlanguage use: a study of style-shifting in morphology and syntax. *Language Learning,* 35, 373-403.

Thomas, H., & James, C. (1999). Incidental vocabulary acquisition in a second language: a review. *Studies in Second Language Acquisition,* 21, 181-193.

Thomas, M. H., & Dieter, J. N. (1987). The positive effects of writing practice on integration of foreign words in memory. *Journal of Educational Psychology,* 79(3), 249-253.

Tomlin, R., & Villa, V. (1994). Attention in cognitive science and second language acquisition. *Studies in Second Language Acquisition,* 16, 183-203.

Trahey, M., & White, L. (1993). Positive evidence and preemption. *Studies in Second Language Acquisition,* 15(2), 181-204.

Treisman, A. (1964). Selective attention in man. *British Medical Bulletin,* 20, 12-16.

Treisman, A. (1979). The psychological reality of levels of processing. In F. C. L. Cermak (Ed.), *Varieties of Attention* (pp.298-326). Hillsdale, New Jersey: Lawrence Erlbaum Associates.

Van den Branden, K. (1994). Evaluating the role of consciousness in second language acquisition: terms, linguistic feature & research methodology.

AILA Review, 11, 27-36.

Van den Branden, K. (1997). Effects of negotiation on language learners' output. *Language Learning,* 47(4), 589-636.

Van Patten, B. (1990). Attending to form and content in the input: an experiment in consciousness. *Studies in Second Language Acquisition,* 12, 287-301.

VanPatten, B. (1993). Grammar teaching for the acquisition-rich classroom. *Foreign Language Annals,* 26, 435-450.

VanPatten, B. (1996). Input processing and grammar instruction. New York: Ablex.

VanPatten, B. (2003). *From Input to Output: A Teacher's Guide to Second Language Acquisition.* New York: McGraw-Hill.

VanPatten, B., & Cadierno, T. (1993). Explicit instruction and input processing. *Studies in Second Language Acquisition,* 15, 225-243.

Verhallen, M., & Schoonen, R. (1998). Lexical knowledge in L1 and L2 of third and fifth grader. *Applied Linguistics,* 19(4), 452-470.

Vermeer, A. (1992). Exploring the second language learner lexicon. In L. V. H. A. L. d. Jong. (Ed.), *The Construct of Language Proficiency* (pp.147-192). Amsterdam: Benjamins.

Vinther, J. (2005). Cognitive processes at work in CALL. *Computer Assisted Language Learning,* 18(4), 251-271.

Vygotsky, L. (1978). Interaction between learning and development. In L. Vygotsky (Ed.), *In Mind in Society* (pp. 79-91). Cambridge, MA: Harvard University Press.

Wang, Q. (2005). *Effects of Semantic Elaboration and Rehearsal on Task-based Vocabulary Acquisition with Corpora.* unpublished thesis. Fujian Normal University, Fuzhou.

Wang, Y. (2005). *Approaches to Enhancing Vocabulary Learning in an EFL Context: A Comparative Study.* unpublished thesis. University of

Toronto, Toronto.

Waring, R. (1999). *Tasks for Assessing Second Language Receptive and Productive Vocabulary*. unpublished thesis. University of Wales, Swansea.

Watanabe, Y. (1997). Input, intake and retention: effects of increased processing on incidental learning of foreign language vocabulary. *Studies in Second Language Acquisition,* 19, 287-307.

Webb, S. (2005). Receptive and productive vocabulary learning: the effects of reading and writing on word knowledge. *Studies in Second Language Acquisition,* 27, 33-52.

Webb, S. (2007). The effects of repetition on vocabulary knowledge. *Applied Linguistics,* 28(1), 46-65.

Wesche, M., & Paribakht, T. S. (1996). Assessing second language vocabulary knowledge: depth versus breadth. *The Canadian Modern Language Review,* 53, 13-40.

White, L. (1989). *Universal Grammar and Second Language Acquisition*. Amsterdam: Benjamins.

White, L. (1990). Second language acquisition and universal grammar. *Studies in Second Language Acquisition,* 12, 121-133.

White, L., Spada, N., Lightbown, P., & Ranta, L. (1991). Input enhancement and L2 question formation. *Applied Linguistics,* 12(4), 416-432.

Widdowson, H. G. (1983). *Learning Purpose and Language Use*. Oxford: Oxford University Press.

Williams, J. N. (1999). Memory, attention, and inductive learning. *Studies in Second Language Acquisition,* 21, 1-48.

Wolter, B. (2001). Comparing the L1 and L2 mental lexicon: a depth of individual word knowledge model. *Studies in Second Language Acquisition,* 23, 41-69.

Wolter, B. (2002). Assessing proficiency through word associations: is there still hope? *System,* 30(3), 315-329.

Wong, W. (2001). Modality and attention to meaning and form in the input. *Studies in Second Language Acquisition,* 23, 345-368.

Wong, W. (2002). Linking form and meaning: processing Instruction. *The French Review,* 76, 236-264.

Wong, W. (2003). Textual enhancement and simplified input: effects on L2 comprehension and acquisition of non-meaningful grammatical form. *Applied Language Learning,* 13, 109-132.

Wong, W. (2004). The nature of processing instruction. In B. VanPatten (Ed.), *Processing Instruction: Theory, Research, and Commentary* (pp. 33-63). Mahwah, NJ: Lawrence Erlbaum Associates.

Wong., W. (2005). *Input Enhancement: From Theory and Research to the Classroom*. New York: McGraw-Hill.

Wong, W. (2007). Processing instruction as input enhancement. In C. Gascoigne (Ed.), *Assessing the Impact of Input Enhancement Is Second Language Education* (pp. 89-106). Stillwater, OK: New Forums Press.

Wu, J. Y. (2005). *Strategies on IELTS: Reading*. Beijing: Higher Education Press. [吴建业，2005. 最新雅思考试胜策：阅读 . 北京：高等教育出版社 .]

Xue, G., & Nation, I. S. P. (1984). A university word list. *Language Learning and Communication,* 3, 215-229.

Zeng, W. X. (2005). Output hypothesis and MIFLI. *Journal of Jianghan University*, 1, 94-99. [曾文雄，2005. 基于输出假设的外语电化教学 . 江汉大学学报（社会科学版）（1）：94-99.]

Zimmerman, C. B. (1997). Do reading and interactive vocabulary instruction make a difference?: an empirical study. *TESOL Quarterly,* 31, 121-140.

Zhang, Q. Z. & Wu, X. Y. (2002). Depths of processing and L2 vocabulary learning. *Modern Foreign Languages*, 2, 176-186. [张庆宗，吴喜燕，2002. 认知加工层次与外语词汇学习——词汇认知直接学习法 . 现

代外语（2）: 176-186.]

Zhang, W. Z. & Wu, X. D. (2003). A cognitive psychological model of L2 lexical competence development in the classroom setting. *Modern Foreign Languages*, 6, 373-384. [张文忠，吴旭东，2003. 课堂环境下二语词汇能力发展的认知心理模式 . 现代外语（6）: 373-384.]

Zhao P. (2004). Reappraisal of the role of input and output in EFL teaching. *Shandong Foreign Languages Teaching Journal*, 5, 68-70. [赵　培，2004. 大学英语教学中“输入”与“输出”角色的重新评估 . 山东外语教学（5）: 68-70.]

Zheng, Y. F. (2005). The output in SLA: A constructivist view. *Journal of Guangzhou University*, 3, 93-96. [郑银芳，2005. 从建构主义角度看二语习得中输出的作用 . 广州大学学报（社会科学版）(3): 93-96.]

Zhou, D. J. & Wen, B. Y. (2000). A track investigation of English vocabulary of Chinese college students. *Foreign Language Teaching and Research*, 5, 356-361. [周大军，文渤燕，2000. 理工科学生的词汇发展状况调查 . 外语教学与研究（5）: 356-361.]

Appendixes

Appendix A   Reading passage one

London Smog

Since the Roman times, if not before, Britain has been known to people abroad as a land of mists and fogs. Until recently, indeed, visitors to the capital could take home with them tins of "London fog"!

For hundreds of years, the mists and fogs of Britain's major cities were all too often polluted and noxious, with London especially badly affected. The fogs impaired health and also posed a threat to travelers who lost their way and thus became an easy prey to robbers. Around 1807, the smoke-laden (充满浓烟的) fog of the capital came to be known as a 'London particular', i.e. a London characteristic. Charles Dickens used the term in *Bleak House* (《荒凉山庄》) and provided graphic descriptions of London's fogs in this and other novels.

The smoke-laden fog shrouded the capital on Friday 5 December 1952 brought premature death to thousands of people and inconvenience to millions. It was estimated that 4,000 people died because of it. Road, rail and air transport were almost brought to a standstill and a performance at the Sadler's Wells Theatre had to be stopped when fog in the hall made conditions intolerable for the audience and performers.

It was not disputed by the medical and other authorities that about 4,000 people were died, but exactly how many people died as a direct result of the fog will never be known. Many who died already suffered from chronic respiratory complaints (呼吸疾病). The fog surely aggravated the disease. Without the fog, those people might not have died when they did. The total number of deaths in Greater London in the week ending 6th December 1952 was 2,062, which was close to normal for the time of year. The following week, the number was 4,703. The death rate peaked at 900 per day on the 8th and 9th and remained above average until just before Christmas. Mortality from bronchitis (支气管炎) and pneumonia (肺炎) increased more than sevenfold as a result of the fog.

The fog of December 1952 was by no means the first to bring death and inconvenience to the capital. On December 27, 1813, the fog was so thick that the mail coach from London to Birmingham took seven hours to reach Uxbridge. It is reported that the fog was so dense that the other side of the street could not be seen. They also tell of the fog bearing a distinct smell of coal tar (煤油). After a similar fog during the week of 7–13 December 1873, the death rate in the Administrative County of London increased to 40 per cent above normal. Acute increases in death rate occurred, too, during the lethal fogs of January 1880, February 1882, December 1891, December 1892 and November 1948. The worst affected area of London was usually the East End, where the density of factories was greater than almost anywhere else in the capital. The area was also low-lying, which inhibited fog dispersing.

As long ago as the 13th century, the hazard of air pollution was recognised as a public-health problem in the cities and large towns of the British Isles, and the burning of coal was identified as the principal source.

请根据课文内容判断下列句子正误：

与原文意思符合请写 T，与原文意思不符请写 F，原文未提及请写 NG。

(　　) One can find the polluted mists and fogs in London because it is known as a 'London particular'.

(　　) The number of people died as a direct result of the fog from December 5 to 9 in 1952 was 4000.

(　　) The fog can disperse easily in the East End in London.

(　　) The specific climate was one of the principal sources of London's noxious fog.

(　　) The lethal fog which would bring death to London mentioned in this article often occurred in winter.

Appendix B Supplementary reading passages

London Smog in 1952

In early December 1952, the weather was cold, as it had been for some weeks. The weather of November 1952 had been considerably colder than average, with heavy falls of snow in southern England towards the end of the month. To keep warm, the people of London were burning large quantities of coal in their grates. Smoke was pouring from the chimneys of their houses and becoming trapped beneath the inversion of an anticyclone (反气旋) that had shrouded over southern parts of the British Isles during the first week of December. Trapped, too, beneath this inversion were particles and gases dispersed from factory chimneys in the London area, along with pollution which the winds from the east had brought from industrial areas on the continent.

During the day on 5 December, the fog was not especially dense and generally possessed a dry, smoky character. When nightfall came, however, the fog thickened. The following day, the sun was too low in the sky to make much of an impression on the fog. That night and on the Sunday and Monday nights, the fog again thickened. In many parts of London, it was impossible at night for walkers to find their way, even in familiar districts. In the Isle of Dogs, the visibility was at times zero. The fog there was so thick that people could not see their own feet! Not until 9 December did it clear. In central London, the visibility remained below 500 metres continuously for 114 hours and below 50 metres continuously for 48 hours. At Heathrow Airport, visibility remained below ten metres for almost 48 hours from the morning of 6th December. The air transport was brought to standstill.

Huge quantities of impurities (杂质) were released into the atmosphere during the period. On each day during the noxious foggy period, the following amounts of pollutants were emitted: 1,000 tonnes of smoke particles, 2,000 tonnes of carbon dioxide. At London's County Hall, the concentration of smoke in the air increased from 0.49 milligrams per cubic meter on 4 December to 4.46 on the 7th and 8th.

The infamous fog of December 1952 has come to be known as 'The Great Smog'; the term 'smog' being a hybrid word meaning 'fog intensified by smoke'. The term was coined almost half a century earlier, by HA Des Voeux, who first used it in 1905 to describe the conditions of noxious fog that occurred all too often over British urban areas. It was popularized in 1911 when Des Voeux presented to the Manchester Conference of the Smoke Abatement League of Great Britain a report on the mortality that occurred in Glasgow and Edinburgh in the Autumn of 1909 as a consequence of lethal fogs.

It was not disputed that the fog of December 1952 was by no means the first to bring death and inconvenience to the capital. On December 27, 1813, the fog was so thick that the mail coach from London to Birmingham took seven hours to reach Uxbridge. It is reported that the fog was so dense that the other side of the street could not be seen. They also tell of the fog bearing a distinct smell of coal tar (煤油). The poisonous fog greatly impaired local residents' health. It also acutely aggravated the chronic diseases. After a similar fog during the week of 7–13 December 1873, the death rate in the Administrative County of London increased to 40 per cent above normal. Acute increases in death rate occurred, too, during the lethal fogs of January 1881, December 1891, and November 1948. The worst affected area of London was usually the East End, where the density of factories was greater than almost anywhere else in the capital. The area was also low-lying, which inhibited fog dispersing.

As long ago as the 13th century, the hazard of air pollution was recognized as a public-health problem in the cities and large towns of the

British Isles, and the burning of coal was identified as the principal source.

请根据课文内容判断下列句子正误：

与原文意思符合写 T，与原文意思不符合写 F，原文未提及写 NG。

1. To keep warm, the people of London were burning large quantities of wood in their houses. (　　)

2. The toxic fog did great harm to local residents' health. (　　)

3. The heavy smog was mainly caused by particles dispersed from local residents' chimneys. (　　)

4. Many local people in London got acute diseases due to the pollution. (　　)

5. The term "smog" was coined in 1952 to particularly refer to the noxious fog in London.(　　)

Reassessment of the Lethal London Fog of 1952

In the last half of the twentieth century, several widely publicized acute episodes of lethal smogs aroused public attention to the hazards of air pollution. One of the earliest such events occurred from 1 December to 5 December 1930 in Belgium. In the last 2 days of the event, more than 60 persons died, which was more than 10 times the normal mortality rate.

The first extreme air pollution episode in the United States took place in Donora, a small town in southwestern Pennsylvania. From 27 October to 30 October 1948, a massive layer of noxious fog shrouded the valley town and brought the town to a standstill. Seventeen people died on Saturday, 30 October, and three more died within the week. The death rate was more than 6 times the norm for the Donora and Webster Hollow area, which had a population of about 14,000. Pollution was so severe that local funeral homes did not have enough coffins and many residents dispersed.

Long known for its foggy weather and coal-burning homes, power plants, and factories, London, England, experienced a dense smog from 5 December to 9 December 1952. According to official government reports, this lethal fog resulted in about 3,000 more deaths than normal during the first 3 weeks of December 1952. With a death rate more than 3 times the norm for this period, the London fog of 1952 is widely regarded as a principal catalyst (催化剂) which aggravated the chronic diseases.

The official report on the London episode by the Ministry of Health noted mortality remained elevated from December 1952 until March 1953 in the region of Greater London. In 1954 Wilkins noted this prolonged increase in mortality and suggested it could be related to air pollution. He also indicated the December 1952 fog might have impaired resistance to illness, causing higher mortality in subsequent months. No follow-up work was done to clarify this idea at the time, and official disputed that the lingering effects of the fog increased rates of illness and death to influenza.

Immediate investigations in Donora, London, and Liege confirmed relationship between short-term reductions in air quality and altered mortality rate. However, no studies were produced within the first several years that addressed persisting public health consequences after each of these episodes.

Since these events, public health researchers have provided extensive documentation that acutely elevated exposures did not cause only acutely evident public health effects, but also aggravated chronic health problems. By extending the period of analysis and looking at novel direct and indirect indicators of respiratory morbidity and mortality for the 3 months after the 1952 London fog, this article establishes that the original assessment was incomplete.

请根据课文内容判断下列句子正误：

与原文意思符合请写 T, 与原文意思不符请写 F，原文未提及请写 NG。

1. The pollution in Donora was so serious that many residents had to leave their hometown to avoid air noxious fog. (　　)

2. It was not until the second half of the twentieth century that people began to pay attention to the harm of air pollution. (　　)

3. The mortality in the region of Greater London began to drop from December 1952 until March 1953. (　　)

4. The december 1952 fog in London might decrease people's resistance to illness. (　　)

5. Mortality might be different because of the change of air quality. (　　)

6. The air would not affect people's health from a long term perspective. (　　)

Appendix C　Sample of instances in COCA

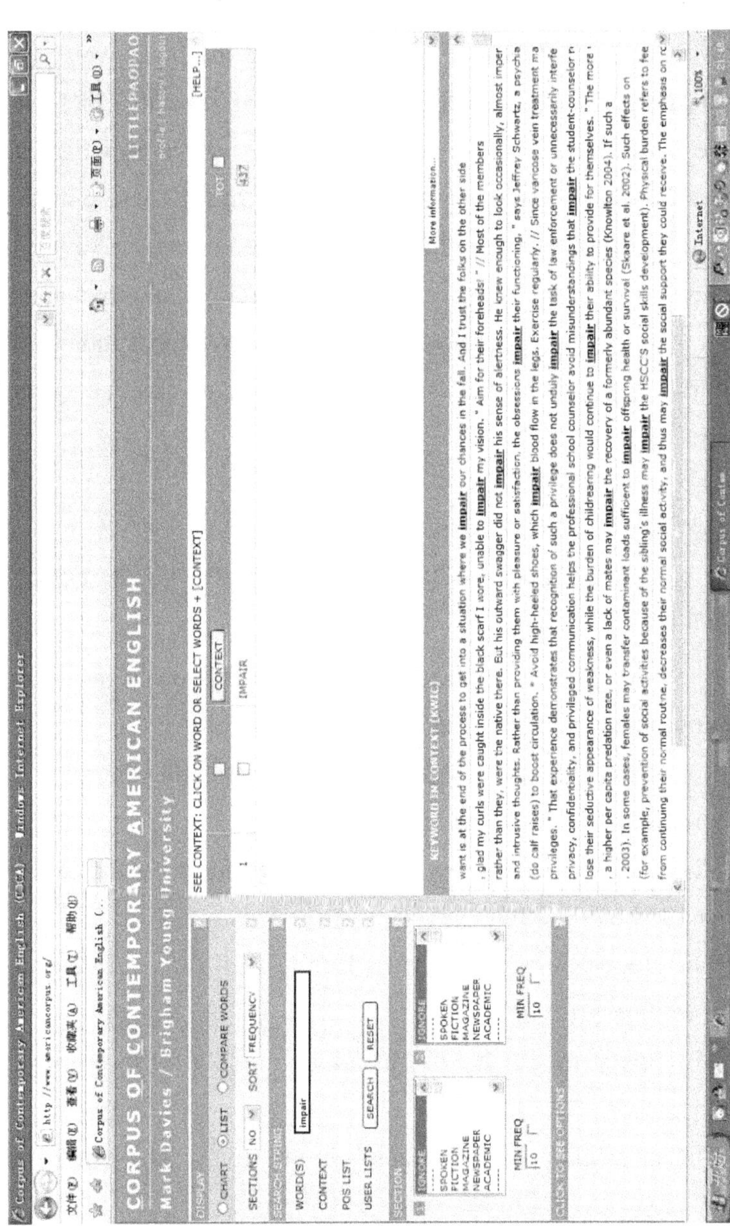

Appendix D　Word note distributed to the inductive group

请通过例句总结出与单词相关的信息。

noxious

词义____________　　词性（　）　词缀（　）

同 / 近义词____________　　反义词____________

搭配________________________

impair

词义____________　　词性（　）　词缀（　）

同 / 近义词____________　　反义词____________

搭配________________________

shroud

词义____________　　词性（　）　词缀（　）

同 / 近义词____________　　反义词____________

搭配________________________

standstill

词义____________　　词性（　）　词缀（　）

同 / 近义词____________　　反义词____________

搭配________________________

dispute

词义____________　　词性（　）　词缀（　）

同 / 近义词____________　　反义词____________

搭配____

chronic
词义________________ 词性 (　　) 词缀 (　　)
同 / 近义词____________ 反义词________________
搭配____

mortality
词义________________ 词性 (　　) 词缀 (　　)
同 / 近义词____________ 反义词________________
搭配____

lethal
词义________________ 词性 (　　) 词缀 (　　)
同 / 近义词____________ 反义词________________
搭配____

disperse
词义________________ 词性 (　　) 词缀 (　　)
同 / 近义词____________ 反义词________________
搭配____

hazard
词义________________ 词性 (　　) 词缀 (　　)
同 / 近义词____________ 反义词________________
搭配____

principal
词义________________ 词性 (　　) 词缀 (　　)

同 / 近义词＿＿＿＿＿＿　　反义词＿＿＿＿＿＿＿＿＿＿
搭配＿＿＿＿＿＿＿＿＿＿＿＿＿＿＿＿＿＿＿＿＿＿＿＿＿

aggravate
词义＿＿＿＿＿＿＿＿　　词性 (　　)　词缀 (　　)
同 / 近义词＿＿＿＿＿＿　　反义词＿＿＿＿＿＿＿＿＿＿
搭配＿＿＿＿＿＿＿＿＿＿＿＿＿＿＿＿＿＿＿＿＿＿＿＿＿

Appendix E　Word list used in the deductive group

noxious(adj.) 词义：<u> 有毒的 </u>
搭配：noxious wastes / gas
例句：
1. The noxious chemical wastes gave great threat to people's health.
2. The factory gave off a great deal of noxious gases.
3. They gave off a most noxious smell.

impair(v.) 词义：<u> 损害，破坏 </u>
搭配：impair one's ability/ health / work
例句：
1. He was mentally impaired after the accident.
2. The illness had impaired his ability to think and concentrate.
3. His heart disease seriously impaired his work.

shroud(v.) 词义：<u> 包裹，覆盖 </u>
搭配：be shrouded in mist / in mystery / in fog
例句：
1. The cliff was shrouded in mist.
2. His work was shrouded in mystery.
3. The city is shrouded in fog.

standstill(n.) 词义：<u> 停 </u>
搭配：came to a standstill/ at a standstill
例句：
1. The program came to a standstill because the shortage of money.

2. Traffic in the city is at a completely standstill.

3. The economy grew slowly or remained at a standstill for long periods, and our people were still living in poverty.

dispute（v.）词义：争论

搭配：dispute about

例句：1. The main facts of the book have never been disputed.

2. They dispute for a long time about the truth of his words.

3. Few would dispute his status as one of the finest artists.

chronic（adj.）词义：慢性的

搭配：chronic illness / problem / shortage

例句：

1. Steen suffers from chronic high blood pressure.

2. There is a chronic shortage of teachers.

3. Water pollution is a chronic problem in this area.

mortality（n.）词义：死亡率

搭配：high/ cancer / adult mortality

例句：

1. Adult mortality from heart disease varies widely across the world.

2. Cancer mortality among older people is high.

3. In this country there is about a twofold difference in mortality for areas of high atmospheric pollution compared with the smoke-free rural areas.

lethal（adj.）词义：致命的

搭配：lethal drug / weapon / chemicals

例句：

1. These chemicals are lethal to fish.

2. Lethal weapon can't be used unless the soldiers' life safety is seriously threatened.

3. His death was directly related to the lethal drug.

disperse（v.）词义：扩散

搭配：cloud / gas disperse

例句：

1. The clouds dispersed as quickly as they had gathered.
2. Police used tear gas to disperse the crowd.
3. You disperse money too liberally

hazard（n.）词义：威胁，冒险

搭配：potential / serious / health hazard

例句：

1. Polluted water sources are a serious hazard to wildlife.
2. Wet roads are a potential hazard to drivers.
3. Eating large meals can be a health hazard.

principal（adj.）词义：主要的

搭配：principal reason / aim / river

例句：

1. His principal reason for making the journey was to visit his family.
2. The principal aim of the policy is to bring peace to the area.
3. The Yellow River is one of the principal rivers of China.

aggravate (v.) 词义：加重，恶化

搭配：aggravate condition / cold

例句：

1. He aggravated his condition by leaving hospital too soon.
2. Mike aggravated his mother just by looking at her.
3. Being out in the rain aggravated his cold.

Appendix F　Reconstruction task for the output group

请根据汉语提示对 “London Smog” 这篇文章进行缩写，括号中为可能用到的生词

（chronic, disperse, lethal, shroud, mortality, hazard, standstill principal noxious, impair, dispute, aggravate）

Since Roman times, if not before, Britain has been known to people abroad as a land of mists and fogs.

____

____

____

____

(数百年来/雾/覆盖/伦敦) Around 1807, the smoke-laden（充满浓烟的）fog of the capital came to be known as a ‘London particular’, i.e. a London characteristic. ____

____

______________________________(雾/污染的/有毒性的/损害/健康)

____

____

____

____________________(致命/大雾/生命/巨大威胁) It was estimated that 4,000 people died because of it. __________________________________

____

____

____

____

__________(医生 / 争论 / 大雾 / 加重 / 病情 / 慢性病病人 / 死亡率 / 上升) Many who died already suffered from respiratory complaints (呼吸疾病). Without the fog, they might not have died when they did. __________ (汽车 / 火车 / 飞机 / 陷入停滞)

The worst affected area of London was usually the East End, where the density of factories was greater than anywhere else in the capital. __________

____

____

____________________(这个地区 / 地势 / 低 / 有害气体 / 难 / 扩散)

____

____

____

____

____

(专家 / 认为 / 烧煤 / 空气污染 / 主要来源)

Appendix G　Vocabulary levels test

This is a vocabulary test. You must choose the right word to go with each meaning. Write the number of that word next to its meaning. Here is an example.

You answer it in the following way.

1. business
2. clock ______6______ part of a house
3. horse ______3______ animal with four legs
4. pencil ______4______ something used for writing
5. shoe
6. wall

Some words are in the test to make it more difficult. You do not have to find a meaning for those words. In the example above, these words are *business*, *clock*, *shoe*.

Try to do every part of the test.

The 2,000-Word Level

1. original
2. private ____________ complete
3. royal ____________ first
4. slow ____________ not public
5. sorry
6. total

1. apply
2. elect ____________ choose by voting
3. jump ____________ become like water

4. manufacture ______________ make
5. melt
6. threaten

1. blame
2. hide ______________ keep away from sight
3. hit ______________ have a bad effect on something
4. invite ______________ ask
5. pour
6. spoil

1. accident
2. choice ______________ having a high opinion of yourself
3. debt ______________ something you must pay
4. fortune ______________ loud, deep sound
5. pride
6. roar

1. basket
2. crop ______________ money paid regularly for doing a job
3. flesh ______________ heat
4. salary ______________ meat
5. temperature
6. thread

1. birth
2. dust ______________ being born
3. operation______________ game
4. row ______________ winning

5. sport
6. victory

The 3,000-Word Level

1. administration
2. angel ______________ managing business and affairs
3. front ______________ spirit who served God
4. herd ______________ group of animals
5. mate
6. pond

1. bench
2. charity ______________ part of a country
3. fort ______________ help to the poor
4. jar ______________ long seat
5. mirror
6. province

1. coach
2. darling ______________ a thin , flat piece cut from something
3. echo ______________ person who is loved very much
4. interior ______________ sound reflected back to you
5. opera
6. slice

1. marble
2. palm ______________ inner surface of your hand
3. ridge ______________ excited feeling
4. scheme ______________ plan

5. statue
6. thrill

1. discourage ________ use pictures or examples to show the meaning
2. encounter
3. illustrate ________ meet
4. knit ________ throw up into the air
5. prevail
6. toss

1. annual
2. blank ________ happening once a year
3. brilliant ________ certain
4. concealed ________ wild
5. definite
6. savage

The 5,000-Word Level

1. alcohol ________ cloth worn in front to protect your clothes
2. apron
3. lure ________ stage of development
4. mess ________ state of untidiness
5. phase
6. plank

1. circus
2. jungle ________ speech given by a priest in a church
3. nomination ________ seat without back or arms
4. sermon ________ musical instrument

5. stool
6. trumpet

1. apparatus ____________ set of instruments or machinery
2. compliment ____________ money received by the government
3. revenue ____________ expression of admiration
4. scrap
5. tile
6. ward

1. bruise ____________ agreement using property as
2. exile security for a debt
3. ledge ____________ narrow shelf
4. mortgage ____________ dark place on your body caused by hitting
5. shovel
6. switch

1. blend
2. devise ____________ hold tightly in your arms
3. embroider ____________ plan or invent
4. hug ____________ mix
5. imply
6. past

1. desolate
2. fragrant ____________ good for your health
3. gloomy ____________ sweet-smelling
4. profound ____________ dark or sad

5. radical
6. wholesome

The University Word List Level

1. affluence
2. axis ____________ introduction of a new thing
3. episode ____________ one event in a series
4. innovation ____________ wealth
5. precision
6. tissue

1. deficiency
2. magnitude ____________ swinging from side to side
3. oscillation ____________ respect
4. prestige ____________ lack
5. sanction
6. specification

1. configuration
2. discourse ____________ shape
3. hypothesis ____________ speech
4. intersection ____________ theory
5. partisan
6. propensity

1. anonymous
2. indigenous ____________ without the writer's name
3. maternal ____________ least possible amount
4. minimum ____________ native

5. nutrient
6. modification

1. elementary
2. negative ______________ of the beginning stage
3. static ______________ not moving or changing
4. random ______________ final, furthest
5. reluctant
6. ultimate

1. coincide ______________ prevent people from doing something they want to do
2. coordinate
3. expel ______________ add to
4. frustrate ______________ send out by force
5. supplement
6. transfer

The 10,000-Word Level

1. acquiesce ______________ work at something without serious intentions
2. contaminate
3. crease ______________ accept without protest
4. dabble ______________ make a fold on cloth or paper
5. rape
6. squint

1. blaspheme
2. endorse ______________ give care and food to
3. nurture ______________ speak badly about God
4. overhaul ______________ slip or slide

5. skid
6. straggle

1. auxiliary		
2. candid	______________	full of self-importance
3. dubious	______________	helping, adding support
4. morose	______________	bad-tempered
5. pompous		
6. temporal		

1. anterior		
2. concave	______________	small and weak
3. interminable	______________	easily changing
4. puny	______________	endless
5. volatile		
6. wicker		

1. dregs	______________	worst and most useless parts of anything
2. flurry		
3. hostage	______________	natural liquid present in the mouth
4. jumble		
5. saliva	______________	confused mixture
6. truce		

1. auspices		
2. casualty	______________	being away from other people
3. froth	______________	someone killed or injured
4. haunch	______________	noisy and happy celebration
5. revelry		
6. seclusion		

Appendix H　VKS Test and 12 Target Words

Sample of the VKS test for the 12 Target words

Impair

I.　我以前从未见过这个单词。

II.　我曾经见过这个单词，但是我不知道它的意思。

III.　我曾经见过这个单词，我想它的意思应该是________.(请给出英文同义词或汉语词义)

IV.　我认识这个词，它的意思是________.(请给出英文同义词或汉语词义)

V.　我可以用这个词造句：________(如果你用此词造句，请务必同时回答第四项)

12 target words:

impair	lethal	mortality	noxious
chronic	dispute	shroud	hazard
aggravate	disperse	standstill	principal

Appendix I Two Supplementary Vocabulary Tests

Dictation test:

请根据录音拼写出单词的正确形式，每个单词读三遍。

______ ______ ______ ______ ______ ______

______ ______ ______ ______ ______ ______

Collocation test:

请从方框里的单词中找出能与下列单词搭配的单词，并构成短语写在对应单词后的横线上。框中单词可重复使用。

1. noxious ____________________
2. disperse ____________________
3. standstill ____________________
4. lethal ____________________
5. shroud ____________________
6. mortality ____________________
7. chronic ____________________
8. aggravate ____________________
9. impair ____________________
10. hazard ____________________
11. dispute ____________________
12. principal ____________________

learning	building	rate	weapon	shorten	fog
come to	gas	health	aim	illness	about